Happily ever after

begins

HERE AND NOW

———————

Living
the
Beatitudes
Today

Happily Ever After
Begins Here and Now

Living the
Beatitudes
Today

BILL DODDS
MICHAEL J. DODDS, O.P.

CHICAGO

Loyola Press Seeker Series
Loyola Press
3441 North Ashland Avenue
Chicago, Illinois 60657

The Seeker Series *from Loyola Press provides trustworthy guides for your journey of faith and is dedicated to the principle that asking questions is not only all right . . . it is essential.*

Series Editor: Jeremy Langford
Cover and interior design: Shawn Biner
Cover photo courtesy of: ©TSM/David Stoecklein, 1996

Library of Congress Cataloging-in-Publication Data
Dodds, Bill.
    Happily ever after begins here and now: living the Beatitudes today/Bill Dodds and Michael J. Dodds.
        p.   cm. -- (Seeker series)
    Includes bibliographical references and index.
    ISBN 0-8294-0970-X (alk. paper)
    1. Beatitudes--Criticism, interpretation, etc. 2. Bible. N.T. Matthew V, 1-12--Criticism, interpretation, etc. 3. Christian life--Biblical teaching. 4. Christian life--Catholic authors.
I. Dodds, Michael J. II. Title. III. Series: Seeker series (Chicago, Ill.)
BT382.D625   1997
241.5'3--dc21   97-12467
                                                          CIP

1 2 3 4 5 / 01 00 99 98 97

To Mom and Dad

Contents

What are the Beatitudes?

When Jesus saw the crowds, he went up the mountain; and after he sat down, his disciples came to him. Then he began to speak, and he taught them, saying:

"Blessed are the poor in spirit, for theirs is the kingdom of heaven.

"Blessed are those who mourn, for they will be comforted.

"Blessed are the meek, for they will inherit the earth.

"Blessed are those who hunger and thirst for righteousness, for they will be filled.

"Blessed are the merciful, for they will receive mercy.

"Blessed are the pure in heart, for they will see God.

"Blessed are the peacemakers, for they will be called children of God.

"Blessed are those who are persecuted for right-eousness sake, for theirs is the kingdom of heaven.

"Blessed are you when people revile you and perse-cute you and utter all kinds of evil against you falsely on my account. Rejoice and be glad, for your reward is great in heaven, for in the same way they persecuted the prophets who were before you."

—*Matthew 5:1–12*

We want to be happy. It's simply part of our human nature. We want to be content. To be at peace.

What we want isn't any different from what the crowds wanted. What the disciples wanted. Some came to Jesus looking for answers. Others were simply curious. Same as us now.

Was it possible this wandering teacher *really* had the answers?

Is it possible this brief collection of sayings really *is* the answer?

We have an advantage over the crowds and the disciples: we know how the Gospels end. On the other hand, the disciples and the crowds had an advantage over us: they understood the commonly accepted definitions for the words Jesus chose to use (which is why this book looks carefully at those particular words). Even so, when he gave them this short list it may have left them a bit overwhelmed and confused.

And, it seems safe to speculate, a little hopeful.

We live in a time when it's easy to feel overwhelmed and confused. We live in a time when Jesus' words about being happy can give us reason to hope.

What does happiness have to do with the Beatitudes?

Some English translations for these verses begin "happy are the poor in spirit," "happy are they who mourn," "happy are the meek," and so on.

By definition, a beatitude is supreme happiness. The word *beatitude* comes from the Latin word, *beatitudo*, which means happiness.

The point here is that when we read the word *blessed*, we need to understand that it means happy, as in complete, made whole, satisfied, and at peace rather than a skewed notion of holy, as in grim, stern, or solemn reverence.

But aren't those who are truly holy—in the best and most accurate sense of the word— truly happy? Of course. That's what the Beatitudes are all about.

That's what Jesus was explaining to his listeners.

"If you *are* this way . . ." or "If this happens to you because you are this way . . ." then you will be given the kingdom of heaven. The earth. Satisfaction. Mercy. And all those other good things.

To whom was Jesus talking? Where and how did he teach?

Imagine two groups. Two concentric circles. In the inner circle are the disciples, Jesus' students. The ones who came to him. The ones he taught.

And in the outer circle are the crowds. The people who had heard things about this fellow and wanted to find out more. Wanted to see for themselves.

"The mountain" certainly wasn't the equivalent of some Rocky Mountain peak. All these people hadn't strapped crampons onto their sandals. We might consider some mountains in the Holy Land nothing more than big hills. But which hill? The Gospel doesn't say although it's clear this mountain is symbolic of Mount Sinai, the place where Moses received the Ten Commandments. (And, not surprisingly, a spot in northern modern-day Israel is, by tradition, "the" place.)

Jesus sat down to teach them. We might imagine him standing up, maybe even hopping up on a nearby boulder so those in the back could see him better. But Oriental—Eastern—teachers generally sat when they taught. And in this case, as he did almost all the time, Jesus—to use a modern phrase—held class outside.

When did Jesus teach this?

The Beatitudes begin what's known as the Sermon on the Mount. It continues to chapter 7, verse 29, and is one of five collections of Jesus' sayings that Matthew has arranged into lengthy talks or discourses.

The equivalent in the Gospel of Luke is the much shorter Sermon on the Plain (Luke 6:20–49). Both begin with the Beatitudes and end with the parable of the house built on rock and the house built on sand.

Luke has four Beatitudes, Matthew has eight. Who's right? Both. Scripture scholars say most likely Luke's first three are "authentic" and the fourth is from the early Church. Matthew has added four based on the Psalms.

But does that mean the Beatitudes in Matthew aren't genuine? Of course not. The verses reflect what Jesus taught his disciples, what the crowds heard, even if we don't know, for example, if he was on a mount or on a plain.

Or if he gave them one-two-three, boom-boom-boom. Or if he limited them to what might be considered these powerful "sound bites."

Despite the differences the two evangelists record, Jesus' message is the same.

What is the message?

Over the past two thousand or so years some of the brightest minds have examined this handful of words, which is why this book includes a sampling of their writings. Overall theories have been presented and debated. Individual nuances of the particular tenses of select words have been expounded on.

At the same time, some of the greatest saints of all time have lived what these twelve verses have taught. They've shown how this short lesson can be used as a blueprint for a holy life—a happy, complete, and blessed life.

Since apostolic times, each generation has rediscovered the Beatitudes. In our own time, the Church noted in its recent catechism that:

> The beatitude [happiness] we are promised confronts us with decisive moral choices. It invites us to purify our hearts of bad instincts and to seek the love of God above all else. It teaches us that true happi-

ness is not found in riches or well-being, in human fame or power, or in any human achievement—however beneficial it may be—such as science, technology, and art, or indeed in any creature, but in God alone, the source of every good and of all love.

In other words, whether we're sitting near Jesus now, paying close attention to the lesson he shares, or standing in that outer ring, curious about what this teacher has to say, we're being offered words that can change our lives. Forever.

Blessed are the poor in spirit, for theirs is the kingdom of heaven

In Scripture

Every age has its own image for making it easier to picture God's power. Ours might have something to do with computers: the ultimate processor, memory, and RAM. Or maybe it's related to quasars, pulsars, and supernovas—the mysterious forces science has discovered far beyond the limits of our galaxy.

In New Testament times, the Jews saw God as an Eastern king. That meant one of his duties was to protect his loyal, but weak, subjects. It was what kings did, it was in their job description. God as protector-king was an easy-to-understand, down-to-earth image because every kingdom then, just as every country now, had its share of poor, defenseless, needy people.

The early Old Testament Hebrew word for the needy was *anawim*. These people weren't living some vague notion of "poverty of spirit," they were downright poor. It wasn't just that they didn't have enough money to buy the goods or services that would have made their lives more comfortable. At times, they didn't have the money to survive.

In modern terms, they are the women, faint with hunger, standing in line at the food banks. They are the men, beat up by misfortune, panhandling on downtown street corners. They are the families, living in their cars, hoping tonight there's going to be room for them at the homeless shelter.

Later on in the Old Testament, the term *anawim* took on a different twist. It was used to describe devout Jews who faithfully observed their religion's many laws.

In Luke's version of the Beatitudes, Jesus is pretty blunt. Blessed are the destitute, theirs is the kingdom of God. Period. Case closed. In Matthew's, Christ cuts people some slack. He adds "in spirit."

So what did that mean? How did that change—amend, modify, soften—the message?

Jesus was telling his listeners they didn't have to live a life of food banks, street corners, and homeless shelters to be a part of God's kingdom. And poor in spirit certainly didn't mean they had to consider themselves dirt, the lowest of the low who should have no sense of self-worth.

To be poor in spirit meant a couple of things. First, Jesus' listeners weren't supposed to focus their lives on making money. Human nature being what it is, it seems safe to say people then, just as people now, thought their lives would be so much easier, so much better, if they just had even a little more cash. Not hit some jackpot, although that would be nice, but just had a little bit more and then—then they would be less preoccupied with material goods. Then they would suddenly become more generous. Then they would be transformed into these wonderful people who . . . (Of course, if a little money did that, a lot of money would be even better, wouldn't it?)

So the first thing Jesus told them—number one on his list so it must have been important for his listeners to hear this—was if they wanted to be happy they couldn't let money remain or become the end-all and be-all of their lives.

His words carried a second message, too. The poor in spirit were those who admitted they were helpless without God, the ones humble enough to accept the fact they weren't in charge.

Relying on, or having a blind love of money (or power, fame, good looks, and so on) wasn't going to bring them the kingdom of heaven. And believing they were in control wasn't going to do it either. Being poor in spirit meant remembering who was the boss—who was the Creator and sustainer of all.

But was the kingdom of heaven something Jesus' listeners would even want? Oh, yes. And it was an idea, a concept, that was so familiar to those folks, he didn't need to explain what it meant. Although, what he meant by the term wasn't what most of them thought it was.

Matthew is the only evangelist who uses the phrase "the kingdom of heaven." (The other synoptic writers, Mark and Luke, prefer "kingdom of God.") In using that phrase, Matthew is following a Jewish custom for showing deep reverence for God. Avoiding saying God's name was a common practice in the first century.

In either case, what did "kingdom of heaven" or "kingdom of God" mean? The phrase goes back to the Old Testament concept of Yahweh—God—as king. The Jews in Jesus' time were very familiar with this, of course, since, with only a few exceptions, the Christian Old Testament is comprised of the Hebrew books of Jewish sacred writing.

The coming of the kingdom of God is at the heart of Jesus' message. It's the good news. Time and again he talked about this. It's central to the explicit prayer he taught his apostles, the Lord's Prayer we still use today. In it we pray "thy kingdom come."

Two things need to be said about this. Two common misconceptions. One has to do with the people of our time, the other with the Jews of the first century.

"Kingdom" isn't always the best translation of what the evangelists wrote because we might tend to think of it as a place. Here are its boundaries. Here are its borders. From here to here, and from here to here, is the kingdom of God. Rather it is the reign of God. It's not a place, but a relationship—all creation truly in harmony with God the creator.

The second misconception, the one that could easily trip up Jesus' followers, is the idea that God's kingdom is an earthly, political one. That Jesus, as the messiah, the anointed one of God, was in the process of establishing a stronghold that would toss the Romans out on their ears. That the kingdom coming meant the days of the Roman army occupying the Jews' homeland were numbered.

Even the apostles sometimes misunderstood. In the first chapter of the Acts of the Apostles, they ask Jesus if *now*, after his crucifixion and resurrection, he plans to "restore the kingdom to Israel" (Acts 1:6). And, of course, they're implying that it would be awfully nice if they could be given cabinet posts in this new administration.

But if the kingdom of God isn't a place, like Monaco, and it doesn't mean giving the Romans the boot, what does it mean? What did Jesus mean when he used that term, which he did time and time again?

This new reign, this long-awaited intervention by God, had arrived. It was there. It had begun. Those who were poor in spirit were going to receive it and be a part of it. At the beginning of his public ministry, Jesus stood up in his hometown synagogue and quoted the prophet Isaiah (61:1): "The Lord God . . . has sent me to bring good news to the oppressed."

Then he told the people that time had come, that time was now (Luke 4:16–20).

The *anawim* had good reason to be happy. Theirs is—not will be—the kingdom of heaven. But—and this is important—at the same time, the kingdom of God is yet to be. This has to do with eschatology, which refers to the branch of theology concerned with the ultimate or final things: death, judgment, heaven, and hell. It's a paradox, a seeming contradiction. The kingdom is here and now and, at the same time, the kingdom will come. It's a tiny seed and growing; at the end of time it will burst into full bloom.

This message, this good news, about the kingdom of heaven was the only promise Jesus repeated in another Beatitude. In fact, it was the one he used to begin and end the traditional eight Beatitudes.

Down through the ages

It's not surprising that down through the centuries prominent doctors of the Church have written about both the poor in spirit and the kingdom of God. And those topics have been addressed in many church documents, including the decrees of the Second Vatican Council.

In his sermon on the Beatitudes, Saint Augustine (354–430) said the opposite of being poor in spirit is falling victim to arrogance and pride. He pretty much called the proud a bunch of windbags.

These people have "high spirits," he noted, and (in some biblical translations) the wind is also called a spirit (Psalm 148:8). They're "puffed up," they're "bloated" by the wind.

Quoting from 1 Corinthians 8:1, Saint Augustine said, "Knowledge puffs up, but charity edifies" (the more modern translation is "knowledge puffs up, but love builds up"). In other words, a self-centered smart aleck (to put it politely) is full of hot air; the person who loves has substance.

That means, Saint Augustine said, it's the humble and God-fearing (those who show God respect) who are poor in spirit. And it's only right that blessedness begins there, he added, referring to Ecclesiastes 1:16 and Psalm 111:10 that say "the fear of the Lord" is the beginning of wisdom.

On the other hand, he pointed out, pride is the beginning of all sin. And he suggested his readers take a look at Ecclesiastes 10:13—"The words of their mouths begin in foolishness, and their talk ends in wicked madness."

Saint Augustine told his readers to let the proud go ahead and strive hard for "the kingdom of the earth." We need to show them love, he suggested, but remember the kingdom of heaven belongs to the poor in spirit. In the sixth century, Pope Saint Gregory I summed it up in one sentence: "Be not anxious about what you have, but about what you are." And choose your companions wisely, suggested Saint Bernard of Clairvaux (c. 1090–1153).

"I wish you to be the friend of the poor," Saint Bernard wrote in his *Letters*, "but especially their imitator. The one is the grade of beginner, the other of the perfect, for the friendship of the poor makes us the friend of kings, but the love of poverty make us kings ourselves. The kingdom of heaven is the kingdom of the poor."

Saint Francis of Assisi (c. 1181–1226) also urged his followers to embrace and love poverty. In this case, not "poverty of spirit" but plain old poverty—"Lady Poverty"—for the sake of the kingdom. A Franciscan motto says "The joy of poverty is not to have nothing in this world; the joy of poverty is to have nothing but God."

A little later, Saint Thomas Aquinas (1225–74) in his *Summa Theologica* referred back to Saint Augustine's image of a "puffed up and proud spirit" and said the person who is poor in spirit is the one who "submits to God."

By that he meant the one who doesn't seek greatness in himself or herself and doesn't seek it in another person. There's no want or demand of the spotlight. There's no blind hero worship. Instead, the one who is poor in spirit looks for greatness only in God.

"Some are strong in chariots," Saint Thomas quoted Psalm 20:8, "some in horses; but we are strong in the name of the Lord, our God." Some, we might say today, care more about their cars than they do about their souls. Or they're brilliant when it comes to technology or making money but lost spiritually.

The poor in spirit aren't caught up in material goods, he explained. They don't need to have the best. They don't seek honors or riches for themselves. Rather, they avoid being puffed up and renounce worldly goods.

In our own time, when the *Catechism of the Catholic Church* talks about "Poverty of Heart," it quotes Vatican II's *Dogmatic Constitution on the Church (Lumen Gentium)*: All of Christ's followers are "invited and bound . . . to guide their affections rightly. Otherwise, they will be thwarted in the search for perfect charity by the way they use earthly possessions and by a fondness for riches which goes against the gospel spirit of poverty."

"The Beatitudes reveal an order of happiness and grace," the catechism continues, "of beauty and peace. Jesus celebrates the joy of the poor, to whom the Kingdom already belongs."

And what is that kingdom? The third-century theologian and scholar Origen said, "Christ is himself the kingdom."

He also pointed out that neither we nor the kingdom is static. It implies and demands our own ongoing transformation. "This Kingdom of God, which we have continually preached in our discourses and writings, we seek to understand it and to become such that we may have God alone as our king and that God's kingdom may became also our own."

Saint Cyril of Jerusalem (c. 315–386) wanted to make it clear Jesus' kingdom would *never* end. In a letter he said, "If ever you hear anyone saying that there is an end to the kingship of Christ, hate the heresy. It is another which has sprouted lately in the region of Galatia."

He was talking about the followers of Marcellus of Ancyra, in what today is Turkey. Marcellians taught that the Incarnation—Jesus becoming a human—was only a temporary transition and that at the end of the world he would return to being only God.

That controversy can seem ancient and obscure but how the Church handled it then is closer than we might realize. In 381 at the Council of Constantinople, the bishops came up with the Nicene-Constantinople Creed (more commonly known as the Nicene Creed). It's the creed usually said at Masses today. And in it, we profess that we believe "his kingdom will have no end."

The words the fourth-century bishops chose, the words we use, reflect the angel's words to Mary at the announcement of Jesus' birth: "he will reign over the house of Jacob forever, and of his kingdom there will be no end" (Luke 1:33).

The thirteenth-century doctor of the Church Saint Albert the Great described the kingdom in three ways. First, it's God reigning in us. Quoting Saint Paul, he said, it's "not eating and drinking, but righteousness, and peace and joy in the Holy Spirit" (Romans 14:17).

But, he went on making his second point, it's also outside us. It's heaven.

And third, it's God, present in both the kingdom within us and the kingdom of heaven. It's God himself.

Martin Luther (1483–1546) taught the kingdom of God was one of grace and mercy; the kingdom of the world a place of anger and harshness. In his "On Temporal Authority," he said human beings are divided between the two. In a sermon he delivered in 1544, he explained, "the worldly government also may be called God's kingdom. For he wills that it should remain and that we should enter it; but it is only the kingdom with his left hand."

The other, Luther said, is God's "right-hand kingdom," where God "himself rules, and is called neither . . . Kaiser nor king . . . but rather is himself." It's there, he added, "the Gospel is preached to the poor."

It wasn't until the nineteenth century that the kingdom of God acquired an immediately recognizable artistic symbol. Edward Hicks (1780–1849), an American Quaker who painted in a primitive style, created many versions of "The Peaceable Kingdom." The scene, based on Isaiah 11:6–8, shows a Delaware River land-scape with the wolf and lamb, leopard and kid, cow and bear, side by side. A lion is eating straw and one child leads them as another plays on the snake's den.

In our own time, Pope John Paul II has written the kingdom is one that "aims at trans-forming human relationships." In his 1991 encyclical letter *On the Permanent Validity of the Church's Missionary Mandate (Redemptoris missio)*, the pope said this kingdom "grows gradu-ally." It does that as "people slowly learn to love, forgive and serve one another." As we become better at listening to Christ's word and following it, the Kingdom of God increases.

John Paul II also explained the kingdom's nature "is one of communion among all human beings—with one another and with God." And because of that, it's the concern of *everyone:* "individuals, society and the world."

To work for the kingdom means "acknowledging and promoting God's activity, which is present in human history and transforms it."

To build the kingdom means "working for the liberation from evil in all its forms."

"In a word," the pope said, "the kingdom of God is the manifestation and realization of God's plan of salvation in all its fullness."

The angel Gabriel told Mary this kingdom was at hand. Now we, in choosing how we live, how we love, and how we become poor in spirit, can play a role in furthering it.

For us today

Is it possible to be poor in spirit now? Yes. Is it easy? No. But then, it never was.

At a time when we divide the globe into first- and third-world nations, most of us in the former are living pretty comfortably. But we never seem to have enough. We always seem to need more money to buy more things.

Being poor in spirit means not caving in to the constant pitch of consumerism. We're its targets and it's very, very good at hitting the mark. That's not surprising. It takes a lot of shots and uses the most sophisticated weapons.

Researchers tell us about the incredible number of television commercials a child sees before even entering kindergarten. Each year news stories report on the millions of dollars corporations spend creating thirty-second spots to be shown during the Super Bowl and on the millions more it takes to air them.

And most advertising doesn't appear to sell a product. It offers us a feeling. A reward. If we lease this car, we'll have great sex appeal. If we buy this beer, our lives will be a never-ending party. If we order this pizza, we'll be so happy. Apparently heaven would be sitting in the car, sipping a brew, and eating a thick-crust pepperoni.

What materialism offers never seems out of reach. We just need to stretch a bit. Spend a bit more money than we wanted to. Spend it a little sooner. Use a little more credit. Go a little deeper in debt.

Where do we draw the line? How do we draw the line? At what point do we say "this is what I need, this is what I have, this is what I want" and realize those are three different categories?

It's tempting to hop on the fast track after beginning a career. But the danger in making that the focus of one's life is that everything else can get blurry. We can easily fail to see what's really important—and what really isn't.

And if we don't draw that line and consciously choose that countercultural lifestyle, it's easy to get sucked into the spend-spend-spend mentality. It's easy to slip from possessing things to being possessed by them.

In recent years the simplicity movement has been helping people draw the line. It's been encouraging people to say not "enough is enough," but "too much is too much." It's helped people come up with an individualized list of what's important and what's not.

Bottom line, it's helped drive home the message things don't matter, people do. The love of things won't bring happiness. The love of people will.

To become poor in spirit, we don't draw a single line. We draw line after line after line. We choose to live simply—again and again and again. We say no to ourselves and to what we want *right now*. Instead, we continue to make do with, be satisfied with, and grateful for what we already have.

But becoming poor in spirit isn't just about our checkbooks. It's about how we see ourselves, how we see others, and how we see our God.

If we're poor in spirit, we know the universe doesn't revolve around us. We know that, while still acknowledging our needs and concerns are important, the needs and concerns of others are important, too.

If we're poor in spirit, we learn how to be of service to others. Not "saving the world," but making a difference where we can. Touching a life at our work, in our home, among our friends, in our community. Saying no to ourselves so we can more easily, more readily, say yes to someone else.

If we're poor in spirit we don't compartmentalize life and religion. We take the time to see how spirituality can't be separated from any human's life. Although sadly, it can be ignored. We can put spirituality on a back burner, or seldom think about it, because God never forces himself on anyone. He loves us so much, so completely, he gives us free will and let's us make the choice.

And what if we do try to choose him? If we do become better at loving others? If we do become less attached to material goods. What then?

Then, Jesus has promised us, ours is the kingdom of heaven. Then we have God's kingdom. Then we become a part of God's kingdom. Then we begin to recognize the reign of God among us and to further it.

If a love of things makes our vision blurry, a love of others and God puts everything in clearer focus. We see ourselves better. See others better.

See God better.

"See God better"? We see him better in what he has created, including the people around us—even when they can't see him in themselves.

But we're not just outside observers or spectators on the sidelines. If we choose to be poor in spirit, we are a part of that kingdom coming. And what a relief that can be!

In the kingdom of heaven, it doesn't matter who has the corner office, who drives the fanciest car, who has the most sophisticated computer or stereo, or who makes the most money. Those goals don't just seem misguided but silly. Foolish.

In the kingdom of God, it doesn't make sense to spend all of one's time and energy to get an office with windows along two walls. To be so concerned about a piece of machinery that will be considered outdated within a year or two, at the most. To live for making money to buy more things that aren't really needed and, after giving ourselves a little time to let an impulse die down, maybe not even really wanted.

But a word of caution: Becoming more in tune and in touch with God's kingdom here and now doesn't mean living in heaven on earth. If we're poor in spirit we still suffer, we still hurt, we still want. We feel incomplete because we are. We weren't made to be here forever. We were created for heaven. We were created to have the ability to choose it.

And we were created so that we can help others choose it, and others can help us. We can be examples to those in our lives who have never heard of being poor in spirit. To those who are looking for answers, looking for peace, but don't realize the only honest answer, the only real peace, comes from being a part of the kingdom of God.

Jesus calls us to be those examples. In the first chapter of the Acts of the Apostles, after his followers asked about the equivalent of cabinet posts in his administration, Jesus told them to be witnesses. He told them the Holy Spirit would fill their hearts, would touch their souls, and would help them take his message, his good news, "to the ends of the earth."

The same can happen in our lives.

By choosing to be poor in spirit, we can become richer than we ever dreamed possible.

To read more about it

Being Poor: A Biblical Study by Leslie H. Hoppe (Wilmington, Del.: M. Glazier, 1987)

Gospel Poverty: Witness to the Risen Christ: A Study of Biblical Spirituality by Michael D. Guinan (New York: Paulist Press, 1981)

The Kingdom of God in History by Benedict Viviano, O.P. (Wilmington, Del.: M. Glazier, 1988)

The Kingdom of God in 20th-Century Interpretation, Wendell Willis, editor (Peabody, Mass.: Hendrickson Publishers, 1987)

Blessed are those who mourn, for they will be comforted

In Scripture

Language has a variety of expressions to describe similar but distinct feelings or experiences. We can feel sad about our team losing a game. We can feel bad we forgot to send a birthday card to a friend. We can feel remorseful about how one of our bad habits has hurt someone we care about. We can feel sorry for a colleague who is going through a rough time. We can feel grief over the death of someone we love. We can mourn for him or her.

Matthew has Jesus using the Greek word *penthein* to describe the people he's talking about in the second Beatitude. In Greek, *penthein* is one of the strongest ways someone can express the feeling of sorrow, of loss, of remorse.

This is someone who has really had the legs knocked out from under him or her. Someone we might expect to be going through the stages author Elisabeth Kübler-Ross in her book *On Death and Dying* describes a terminally ill person experiencing: denial, anger, bargaining, depression, and so on.

Penthein was usually used to refer to someone who was mourning the death of a loved one. Someone numb, someone in shock, someone feeling a gaping hole in his or her heart.

The Old Testament speaks of mourning with the death of Sarah, wife of Abraham (Genesis 23:2). The widower, we're told, "went in to mourn for Sarah and to weep for her." What did that mean? There's no list of specifics but we do know some of the traditions. For example, survivors used ritual lamentation—dirges—as a part of their mourning (2 Samuel 1:17–27).

Someone who was mourning might wear sackcloth (a rough fabric made of woven hair that was used for a number of things, including bags for grain), wipe dust on his or her head, or walk barefoot. Joy was shown by washing, by anointing with oil, by wearing a clean— what we might call "Sunday best"—garment. Expressing sorrow was doing the opposite. It was getting dirty, donning old clothes, and shouting traditional cries of grief.

What else does the Old Testament say about mourning, about grieving? Psalm 30— offering "thanksgiving for recovery from grave illness"—exults "You have turned my mourning into dancing; you have taken off my sackcloth and clothed me with joy." Ecclesiastes 3:4 tells people there's "a time to weep, and a time to laugh; a time to mourn, and a time to dance."

The book of Sirach advises "do not avoid those who weep, but mourn with those who mourn" (7:34). In Isaiah 61:1–2, the Lord makes the same promise Jesus does in the second Beatitude: "He has sent me . . . to comfort all who mourn."

Does this mean Christ was referring to only those who are grieving over the death of a friend or family member? No. His description includes those who hurt physically. Those in pain because of an ailment, a disabling condition, a chronic disease.

It includes those who are hungry. Those who are homeless. Those who are persecuted.

It includes those who are without hope. Those suffering from depression. Those who are mentally ill.

It includes those who feel the pain of others. Those who try to ease that pain, erase that pain, but know they can't end all the suffering that is a part of this world.

It includes those who feel an aching remorse for their own sins. Those in sorrow for the times they turned away from their heavenly Father. Turned their backs on their brothers and sisters.

And it includes those who hurt because the life they want to lead isn't the life they're leading as they stumble again and again, unable to match Christ's example of true love.

The Gospels tell us Jesus knows the pain we feel and he is moved with compassion (Mark 6:34, 8:2). The powerful Greek word used to describe his empathy is *splagchnizestha*. The *splagchna* are the bowels. *Splagchnizestha* is what we might call a gut feeling. Something we experience down in our souls.

It's not surprising then that what Jesus promises for those who are mourning is more than simply a sympathetic pat on the back. The word that's used—*parakalein*—does mean to comfort or to console but it's not just limited to that.

Jesus is inviting them to a banquet. Jesus is saying, yes, God will give those who mourn comfort and consolation but he will also invite them not just into his home but to his very table. They will be his guests, his friends.

Further still, the word means those who mourn are being called on to become God's helpers—to become witnesses to the truth Jesus is preaching, to become his allies in spreading this Good News. How can these downtrodden do that? *Parakalein,* the word Jesus uses, not only means to comfort, it also means to encourage, to excite, and to urge. Those who mourn can now be his witnesses because of God's unmatchable courage.

Just as the once timid apostles burst forth from hiding after the Holy Spirit (the Paraclete, the comforter) descended on them on Pentecost (Acts 2:1–4), those who mourn will have their hearts set on fire. They will have—to use another modern phrase—"the fire in the belly" to become those allies, those witnesses.

And as with the word *mourning, comfort* also can be found throughout Scripture. (Our English word *comfort* is used in the Bible more than fifty times. *Mourning* appears three times as often as that.) Sometimes that comforting is a family gathering to console one member, especially after the death of a loved one (1 Chronicles 7:22). But then, too, there are times when it's an individual asking God for help (Psalm 119:82) or thanking him for already providing it (Isaiah 52:9).

At other times in the Bible the burden is more on those who are praying. God asks us to console one another: "Comfort, O comfort my people, says the Lord" (Isaiah 40:1).

And at times, with an image and promise that continues to encourage and console people today, God vows that "as a mother comforts her child, so will I comfort you; you shall be comforted in Jerusalem" (Isaiah 66:13).

Down through the ages

Is it better to laugh with the sinners than cry with the saints? That was the point singer-songwriter Billy Joel was making a number of years ago in his "Only the Good Die Young."

Gregory of Nyssa, a Father of the Church who lived from 330 to 394, said that's not true. In fact, Gregory claimed the opposite. Those laughing sinners, he said, are dumb as cattle. They don't even know what they're missing and so they never even look for it.

But what is "it"? Gregory used the Philosophy 101-sounding term "the Good."

"The more we believe the Good of its very nature lies far beyond the limits of knowledge, the more we experience a feeling of sorrow that we must be separated from so great and desirable Good and cannot even encompass it with our minds," he wrote. In other words, the more we come to realize that our true happiness lies beyond all the world has to offer, the sadder we become at our separation from it.

Speaking specifically about the second Beatitude, Gregory said when Jesus told his listeners that those who mourn are blessed, the "hidden lesson" he was teaching was—to use a modern expression—to keep your eyes on the prize.

If we become distracted by the flash and glitter of the world we will never find the Good. If we become consumed chasing the flash and glitter, we may fail to learn there even is the Good.

No, Gregory said, the way to true happiness is to mourn the fact we don't have the Good. And to use our mourning as a foundation—or better still a springboard—to begin searching for it.

But can we start to look without first being in mourning? Gregory didn't think so. It would be impossible for us to live "without tears" if we looked closely at the reality of our human lives. And when we do that, we can't help but feel pity for those who can't see beyond the world's pleasures.

Why? Because the Good we seek is communion with God. The more we are aware of our lack of such communion, the more we mourn its absence. That's what hurts so much.

Added to that is the sorrow of seeing others who are not even looking for God because they don't know God is what they need. Gregory compared them to animals that romp and stomp all day not even realizing they lack the ability to reason. Lack the power to think. Lack the power to freely choose.

They're so content because they don't have a clue of what they're missing. But if they did know . . . how could they help but feel terrible?

Does all this mean our lives are futile? On the one hand, we might not even know we're missing something and so remain pathetic. On the other, if we do realize the rift in our relationship with God, we always feel miserable.

But that's not the case. Why? Because "all will be well, and all will be well, and all manner of things will be well." That's a popular quotation from the mystic Julian of Norwich (1342–1416). In her book *Showings*—meaning visions—she offers words of consolation and encouragement.

When she was talking about seeing the pain of the world, she noted, "I do not see sin." That was because she believed that sin "has no substance or real existence. It can only be known by the pain it causes."

Julian said she could see that pain, but it doesn't last forever. And "it purges us and makes us know ourselves, so that we ask for mercy."

What Julian was expressing is the traditional interpretation of this Beatitude. We mourn because we are sinners and in doing so discover God's mercy, God's comfort. "Our comfort against all this [pain]," she wrote, is "the passion of Our Lord . . . for such is his blessed will."

Christ offers comfort "at once and sweetly" because of his tender love for us. She wrote that it is as if he's telling us "it is true that sin is the cause of all the pain; but it is all going to be all right . . . all right . . . all right." In Julian's vision, "these words were said most tenderly, with never a hint of blame either to me or to any of those to be saved."

But beyond that, she continued, the next step after her seeing Christ's compassion for us and feeling her own sorrow and compassion at the sight of his suffering, was being "filled with compassion for all my fellow Christians, these people greatly beloved and saved, the servants of God."

In talking about the suffering we all endure in this world, Julian said now she could understand how Jesus rejoiced in the "tribulations of his servants, though with pity and compassion."

"To bring them to bliss," she wrote, "he lays on each one he loves some particular thing, which while it carries no blame in his sight causes them to be blamed by the world, despised, scorned, mocked and rejected."

He does that, she continued, "to forestall any hurt they might get from the pomps and vanities of this sinful world, to prepare their way to heaven, and to exalt them in his everlasting bliss."

Julian said that Jesus told her in a vision "I shall wholly break you of your empty affections and your pernicious pride. Then I shall gather you together, and by uniting you to myself make you humble and mild, clean and holy."

The reason we can feel compassion for others, the mystic also wrote, is because Christ is in us. And, she added, "we do not suffer on our own" but with Christ. And his "suffering and self-abnegation so far surpasses anything we might experience that we shall never fully understand it."

If we can begin to see these things, she taught, we'll "stop moaning and despairing about our own sufferings."

"We can see that our sin well deserves it," Julian said, "but that his love excuses us. In his great courtesy he overlooks the blame, and regards us with sympathy and pity, children both innocent and loved."

In our own era, a German Lutheran theologian and minister who had written about suffering (and the Beatitudes) came face to face with it in a way that was like no other in the twentieth century. Adamantly opposed to Hitler and the Nazi regime, Dietrich Bonhoeffer (1906–45) was hanged in a concentration camp after spending two years in prison.

In his *The Cost of Discipleship* written in 1937, Bonhoeffer taught that with each Beatitude, "the gulf" widened between Christ's disciples and all others. And when Jesus spoke of mourning, he meant "of course, . . . doing without what the world calls peace and prosperity. . . . Refusing to be in tune with the world or to accommodate oneself to its standards."

Those who are able to do that, Bonhoeffer wrote, "mourn for the world, for its guilt, its fate and its fortune."

They grieve, the minister said, while the world dances.

They see the ship is sinking . . . while the band plays on.

The world focuses all its attention on progress, power, and the future, he wrote, "but the disciples meditate on the end, the last judgment, and the coming of the kingdom." That's why Christ's followers find themselves "strangers in the world, unwelcome guests and disturbers of the peace."

"No wonder," Bonhoeffer added, "the world rejects them!" And while they don't go looking for that rejection "by adopting an attitude of contempt or disdain," they don't run from it either.

The theologian said he liked the word Martin Luther used for mourn: *Leidtragen,* meaning sorrow-bearing. The Christian community "does not shake off sorrow as though it were no concern of its own, but willingly bears it." And in doing so, its members "show how close are the bonds which bind them to the rest of humanity."

For us today

We only end up feeling frustrated if we fall into the trap of believing "happily ever after" can be experienced completely here and now. If we hold our breath waiting for all the tumblers to fall into place and the door to swing open to absolute contentment.

It's impossible to get through life without feeling pain. Without feeling disappointment. Without feeling grief.

It's impossible to get through life without being hurt by others. Without making costly mistakes. Without sinning and suffering the here-and-now consequences of those sins.

Does that mean there's no reason to hope? That religion really is nothing more than a promise of pie in the sky, by and by? No.

To those who would argue it's senseless to believe in a God when there's so much suffering in the world, this Beatitude answers that without a God so much suffering would make no sense. It says that those who mourn—and we all fall into that category at times—have the opportunity, the ability, to more clearly see reality, to more surely head toward our loving Creator.

How can that be? Our lives are filled with examples. In times of crisis, we turn—or return—to God in prayer. When our parent, our child, our spouse, our friend faces serious illness or is hurt in a devastating accident. When personal financial disaster looms. When drug or alcohol abuse is crushing the life out of us. When, to quote the twenty-third Psalm, we "walk through the darkest valley" (sometimes translated "the valley of the shadow of death").

When circumstances bring us face-to-face with the realization that in many ways we aren't in control of our lives and our "best laid plans" can, in an instant, turn to dust. And admitting that's possible in one area of our lives often brings with it the realization the same is true in so many others. If one of our parents is seriously ill and facing surgery, the other seems much more fragile and vulnerable. If this friend has been the victim of violence then others close to us could be, too.

This is a truth we can easily forget or overlook when we're caught up in pursuing what the world has to offer (the money, the power, the status). We lose sight of the fact we're all fragile, we're all vulnerable. There is no guarantee who among us will be here tomorrow, and who will be gone forever.

It isn't surprising then that not infrequently it's those who have been kicked around by life who don't sweat the small stuff. They are the ones who—in the same way a wise person picks his or her fights carefully—pay particular attention to where and how they give their heart, give their souls.

It isn't surprising then that not infrequently a young person, a child even, who has lived with suffering has a spiritual wisdom and strength and certitude far beyond his or her years. This is the young man with AIDS who finds himself comforting his friends. This is the little girl with cancer who ends up consoling her parents.

If our own suffering, our own times of mourning, can in some way—even a small way—give us these same God-given gifts if we would only accept them, why do we hesitate to do so? As is so often the case, we stumble over our own pride and we put an intellectual spin on our falling. We don't want to be "hypocrites." We don't want to, just because times have gotten rough, turn our backs on our own theological code. A code which may be agnostic, if not atheistic.

We think it just wouldn't be right to suddenly come running to God because life's problems seem overwhelming. Jesus says the opposite. That's a *great* time to come running to God. There's no such thing as a bad time, an inappropriate time, to come running to God. Like the father of the prodigal son (Luke 15:11–32), our heavenly Father waits for us. Is on the lookout for us. Will come rushing out to greet us if we take even a small step toward him.

Our heavenly Father loves us so much he has given us the power to make that choice. To turn our backs on him or turn our hearts toward him. We're not animals romping in the field, although we can choose to live like them. We can fail to think beyond material things in front of our noses (the new car, the nicer house, the immediate pleasure, whatever it might be). We can fail to think beyond our own needs, our own desires.

Or we cannot only accept and grow from our own times of mourning, but offer comfort to those around us who are hurting. We can search out the mournful and, if not take away their pain, at least be there with them as they endure it.

We can choose—as Christ showed us how we serve him by serving others—to feed the hungry, to welcome the stranger, to care for the ill, to visit the imprisoned (Matthew 25:31–45).

Exercising our free will, we have the ability—right here and right now—to comfort those who mourn. And they are all around us. They fill our world.

And in doing so we will add to our own sorrow as we come to better realize that no matter how much we do to help, no matter how good we are at helping, there will still be pain in this imperfect world. There will always be mourning.

We will come to better realize how far short we fall from the person we want to be. The person we were created to be. How much and how frequently we hobble ourselves by sin. How what we were created to be and who we were created to be will never be fully realized on earth.

And so we will discover this new reason to mourn—for ourselves and for those among us who never look beyond their next pleasure.

But we will also begin to discover the amazing truth that, to quote the *Catechism of the Catholic Church*, it's possible for "suffering, a consequence of original sin," to "acquire a new meaning." It's possible for suffering to become "a participation in the saving work of Jesus." We will begin to see that through our suffering we can "unite" ourselves "more closely with Christ's passion" and start to understand how and why Paul could write "I am now rejoicing in my sufferings for your sake" (Colossians 1:24).

We will have the opportunity to find comfort and hope in the middle of our own suffering as we more easily and effectively offer that same comfort and hope to those around us who are hurting.

And we will have the opportunity to become better witnesses. The opportunity to grow stronger as Christ's allies. The opportunity to more clearly hear God's invitation to join him at the eternal banquet where, to quote Revelation 21:4, "he will wipe every tear" from our eyes and "death will be no more; mourning and crying and pain will be no more."

To read more about it

The Cost of Discipleship by Dietrich Bonhoeffer (New York: Macmillan, 1963)

Making Sense Out of Suffering by Peter Kreeft (Petersham, Mass.: St. Bede's Publications, 1986)

Showings by Julian of Norwich (New York: Paulist Press, 1978)

Blessed are the meek, for they will inherit the earth

In Scripture

It's easy to understand why this Beatitude isn't too appealing these days. Meekness tends to be viewed as a weakness rather than a virtue. A different, and more accurate, way of looking at this verse is to see that it has to do with anger. It doesn't ask a Christian to never get mad, but to use his or her anger wisely and well.

In Scripture, the Greek *praus*, meaning meek or gentle, referred to a person who had a positive attitude toward God and others, not to someone who had no self-esteem or backbone. Who was meek? In the Old Testament, "the man Moses was very humble, more so than anyone else on the face of the earth" (Numbers 12:3). In the New Testament, Jesus told the people, "Take my yoke upon you, and learn from me, for I am gentle and humble in heart, and you will find rest for your souls" (Matthew 11:29).

Learn from me. I am meek. This must be a good thing. It wasn't how others were describing Christ. This is what he was saying about himself. It was meekness that allowed Jesus to pray to his Father in the Garden of Gethsemane "Not what I want but what you want" (Matthew 26:39). It was meekness that allowed him to say, even in his agony, "your will be done" (Matthew 26:42).

Jesus' meekness meant that he could accept God's will, whatever that might be, that he would be obedient to the Father, that he would trust him.

In Scripture, to be meek was to be someone who didn't become angry with God or bitter because of what life may bring. (And, referring back to the previous Beatitude, any life is certain to have sadness and disappointment.) To be meek was to believe goodness — growth and grace — could come from any calamity. To believe God really was in control and, as Julian of Norwich later expressed it, "all will be well."

But, again, to be meek didn't mean being a zombie; it didn't mean never getting angry. Rather, it was knowing when to get angry, and how to get angry.

What made Jesus mad? The self-righteous he called hypocrites and "whitewashed tombs," those fixed up nicely on the outside but filled with decay on the inside (Matthew 23:27). The sleazy merchants who squeezed money out of the common folk who came to the temple to pray. Still meek, he made "a whip of cords . . . drove all of them [the merchants] out of the temple" and "poured out the coins of the money changers and overturned their tables" (John 2:15).

It was clear he was ticked.

What *didn't* make Jesus mad? When others called him names or tried to trick him. When leaders plotted to arrest him. When one of his own betrayed him with a kiss and another three times denied even knowing him.

As someone meek, Jesus had the ability to be angry but not sin (which was the challenge — the admonition — Paul stressed in his letter to the Ephesians [4:29]). As someone meek, Jesus lived his life in balance, never straying to either negative extreme—destructive rage or wimpiness.

And, he promised, those who followed along the same path, followed in his footsteps, would "inherit the land."

When Jesus said this he was quoting Psalm 37 which describes the fate of sinners and the reward of the just. Trust in God, the psalmist says again and again, and know the wicked are going to have to pay the price of their sinfulness. It's in verse 11 that the just are told "the meek shall inherit the land" and "delight . . . in abundant prosperity."

What land? Where? And what did inherit mean?

Both the Old and New Testament are filled with references to inheritance. Sometimes it had to do with a person's property and possessions, such as when Sarah let Abraham know, in no uncertain terms, their son Isaac was getting *everything*. There would be no sharing with Ishmael, the son he had had with his slave Hagar (Genesis 21:10).

And sometimes it referred to Yahweh's promise to the Hebrews enslaved in Egypt. He was going to lead them to "a land flowing with milk and honey." There they would receive "fields and vineyards" for their "inheritance" (Numbers 16:14).

So in the legal sense, inheritance had to do with who got what when a parent died. All the sons got something, even illegitimate ones or ones born of slaves, which was what Sarah was complaining about. The eldest son would receive a double portion, twice the size of the other brothers. For instance, if a father had three sons, the land would be divided into fourths. The younger sons would each receive one quarter of the property and the eldest would get one half. Also, the eldest would become head of the household. While a father couldn't change this rule, even if one of the younger boys was his favorite or was better suited or more worthy of the greater share, some dads didn't follow it (for example, Jacob with Joseph or David with Solomon).

What about women? A widow was given nothing. If she went back to her father's house, the dead man's property went outside the family. Daughters received no inheritance because it would pass out of the family to their husbands. A later law said that if a man died with no sons, the list of succession was daughters, brother, paternal uncle, nearest male relative. A refinement added that a daughter who inherited had to marry within the tribe, to keep the property within it.

All that had to do with laws, property, and material goods. At the same time, theologically speaking, inheritance in the Old and New Testaments came to mean something else. In the Old Testament, God promised the Israelites that as his chosen people, they would come to inherit and possess that "land of milk and honey." This wasn't an abstract concept, this was Canaan. A place where the nomadic tribes of Israel would settle down and stay, where each would receive its appropriate portion. While the story of the Israelites shows they didn't simply waltz into this territory and have it handed to them, they understood it wasn't because of their great military skill that they came to possess it. As an inheritance, it became theirs because God gave it to them.

But, even in the Old Testament and certainly throughout the New, the promised land came to mean something else, something more, something even better. In the Old Testament, the promise was the coming of the Messiah, the anointed one of God, who would usher in the new kingdom. In the New Testament, this land Jesus was talking about and promising to his followers in the third Beatitude was the kingdom. The inheritance he offered (and offers still) was salvation and eternal life. And he freely handed it to not only the Jews (the blood-line descendants of the twelve tribes) but the Gentiles.

The meek can inherit this land, this promise. They can become a part of this kingdom of heaven which (as talked about in chapter 2) is both here and now and still to come.

Down through the ages

When Saint Augustine wanted to describe the meek he said they were the ones "who submit to iniquities and do not resist evil, but overcome evil with good."

The haughty can go on fighting about "earthly and temporal things," he wrote in his commentary on the Sermon on the Mount, but the meek "'shall inherit the land'—the land from which they cannot be expelled."

Saint Gregory of Nyssa stressed that being meek wasn't the same as being calm and listless. "For if," he said, "by this expression is meant everything is done quietly and slowly, I do not think one should indiscriminately consider virtuous whatever is done in meekness."

He maintained that to be meek was to be the strong, talented athlete Paul referred to in his first letter to the Corinthians (9:24–27)—one who exercises "self-control in all things," one who does not "run aimlessly," one who does not "box as though beating the air." Gregory wrote, "Speaking of our race for the prize of our heavenly vocation, Paul advises us to increase our speed: 'So run,' he says, 'that you may obtain.'"

On the other hand, meekness is also a slowing down but not just any slowing down. According to Gregory, we humans tend to speed up—like rocks rolling down a hill—when we're giving in to our lower impulses. And because "our nature is very quick to turn toward evil, slowness and quiet in these matters are called blessed."

Saint Thomas Aquinas taught "meekness mitigates the passion of anger." Meekness tempers angers, controls it, channels it. It does not suppress anger, but allows for the healthy exercise of anger.

Saint Thomas said, "Meekness moderates anger by subjecting it to right reason." The one who is meek is not dominated by his or her anger, but sees and deals with anger from a new perspective, the broad and encompassing picture of one's life and relationships that Saint Thomas calls right reason.

Unchecked anger can be a cause of blindness in our relation with God and other people. Meekness lets us see the truth about these relations. As Saint Thomas put it, "Anger is, on account of its impetuousness, a very great obstacle to one's free judgment of truth; so meekness, which mitigates anger, makes one self-possessed. So it is written, 'My son, keep your soul in meekness' (Sirach 10:28)."

Meekness makes us self-possessed—lets us see the truth about ourselves that we miss when we're dominated by anger. It also lets us hear the truth of God's word to us and about us, which our anger can distort or ignore. "It pertains to meekness that one does not contradict the words of truth, which many do through being disturbed by anger," Saint Thomas noted. "So Augustine says, 'To be meek is not to contradict Holy Writ, whether we understand it, if it condemn our evil ways, or understand it not, as though we might know better and have a clearer insight of the truth.'"

That means if we are meek, then we are open to God's word, not rejecting it when it challenges us to change, and not thinking that we know better than our Creator what is good for us—what will truly lead us to life and joy.

To put it in modern and simpler terms, the person who is meek never falls into a blind rage. It's easier for the meek person to live the truth because he or she never loses sight of the truth. That person doesn't seek revenge since he or she more clearly understands and so more readily empathizes with others.

"Who are 'the meek'?" asked John Wesley (1703–91), the English theologian and evangelist and the founder of Methodism. He answered his own question in a series of sermons on the Beatitudes.

They aren't those "who grieve at nothing, because they know nothing; who are not discomposed [agitated] at the evils that occur, because they discern not evil from good. Not those who are sheltered from the shocks of life by a stupid insensibility; who have, either by nature or art, the virtue of stocks [stumps] and stones, and resent nothing, because they feel nothing."

To be meek is not to be numb because "apathy is as far from meekness as from humanity." And it doesn't mean "being without zeal for God."

No, he wrote, "Christian meekness . . . keeps clear of every extreme, whether in excess or defect. It does not destroy but balance the affections, which the God of nature never designed should be rooted out by grace, but only brought and kept under due regulations. It poises the mind aright. It holds an even scale, with regard to anger, and sorrow, and fear; preserving the mean in every circumstance of life, and not declining either to the right hand or the left."

Meekness, then, is like an inner ear, keeping us balanced. It's like a thermostat, making sure we never become too hot or too cold.

Meekness is a virtue, Wesley wrote, that has to do with our relationship with God and with others. "When this due composure of mind has reference to God, it is usually termed resignation; a calm acquiescence in whatsoever is his will concerning us, even though it may not be pleasing to nature; saying continually, 'It is the Lord; let him do what seemeth him good.' When we consider it more strictly with regard to ourselves, we style it patience or contentedness. When it is exerted toward other men, then it is mildness to the good, and gentleness to the evil."

The meek can see what is evil, Wesley said, and they can suffer from evil but "still meekness holds the reins."

"Their zeal is always guided by knowledge, and tempered, in every thought, and word, and work, with the love of man, as well as the love of God," he said. "They do not desire to extinguish any of the passions which God has for wise ends implanted in their nature; but they have mastery of all: They hold them all in subjection, and employ them only in subservience to those ends."

That's why he taught, "even the harsher and more unpleasing passions are applicable to the noblest purposes; even hatred, and anger, and fear, when engaged against sin, and regulated by faith and love, are as walls and bulwarks to the soul, so that the wicked one cannot approach to hurt it."

A century after Wesley, Thérèse of Lisieux (1873–97) showed even saints have difficulty with this virtue because in everyday life some people just *bug* us. And it's only with great effort that meekness is possible.

In her autobiography, *Story of a Soul,* the young Carmelite wrote that in the convent "no one has enemies, but one certainly has natural likes and dislikes. One feels attracted to a certain sister and one would go out of one's way to dodge meeting another."

Thérèse had a particular colleague in mind. "Jesus tells me that it is this very sister I must love," she explained, "and I must pray for her even though her attitude makes me believe that she has no love for me."

Who was this thorn in Thérèse's side that challenged her ability to remain meek, remain "balanced"? It was a community member "who managed to irritate me whatever she did or said."

"As I did not want to give way to my natural dislike for her, I told myself that charity should not only be a matter of feeling but should show itself in deeds," Thérèse noted. "So I set myself to do for this sister just what I should have done for someone I loved most dearly. Every time I met her, I prayed for her and offered God all her virtues and her merits. . . . I did not remain content with praying a lot for this nun who caused me so much disturbance. I tried to do as many things for her as I could and whenever I was tempted to speak unpleasantly to her, I made myself give her a pleasant smile."

But Thérèse admitted that when she couldn't muster up a big smile, she would slip away quickly, fleeing "like a soldier deserting the battlefield."

What, over time, was the result? "After all this she asked me one day with a beaming face: 'Sister Thérèse, will you please tell me what attracts you so much to me? You give me such a charming smile whenever we meet.' Ah! It was Jesus hidden in the depth of her soul who attracted me, Jesus who makes the bitterest things sweet."

Through her continued meekness, Thérèse had begun to "inherit the earth," to enter more into Christ's kingdom, to more easily recognize him here and now.

"Jesus does not demand great deeds," she concluded. "All he wants is self-surrender and gratitude."

For us today

These days a commonly held interpretation of "the meek will inherit the earth" is if we're not, at all costs, number one, we end up somewhere in the back of the herd eating a lot of people's dust. Or, as one song from the musical *Camelot* puts it: "It's not the earth the meek inherit; it's the dirt."

Meekness is considered—at best—silly, if not downright harmful.

And if that's the case, why would anyone want to be meek, much less work at becoming *more* meek? He or she would have to have a screw loose, have zero self-esteem, or be some kind of masochist.

That point of view makes sense if we're talking about the standard definition of the English word *meek*. Yes, a dictionary may say first it means showing patience and humility or being long-suffering but in common use it means being submissive, being easily imposed on, being spineless. The word itself comes from the Old Norse meaning soft. Only in its archaic definition does meek mean kind or gentle.

It's a shame that we don't use a word that more accurately reflects what Jesus was talking about in his third Beatitude—a pity *meek* now has such a negative spin to it. Why? Because our time, our society, certainly could use a large dose of meekness. And *we* would be better off—healthier, happier, holier—if we were more meek.

Does that seem farfetched?

Consider society first. We have a population dotted with people who are trying to live their lives at the extremes. On the one end is the person consumed with rage, the one who can't control his or her anger.

When someone cuts ahead of him on the freeway, he speeds up behind the offending car and dangerously tailgates as he lays on the horn and thrusts his hand in an obscene gesture. Or when her young child commits some offense, no matter how slight, she clobbers him.

This is the individual who, after taking real or imagined abuse at the workplace or school for months or years, walks into the building with a gun and begins firing at anyone who moves or at anyone who doesn't.

And at the other end of this spectrum is the person who acts like a doormat, the person who takes abuse for months or years and instead of speaking up, instead of facing and dealing with the problem he or she swallows the anger and frustration. And as time goes by it seems to eat a hole in his or her stomach, pride, health, life. It causes not just emotional pain but leads to actual physical ailments. Ignoring that constant stress and the basic instinct to fight or flee takes a heavy toll.

Certainly we've come across people like this. Certainly there have been times when, to one degree or another, we were one of them.

What would meekness do for those people at the extremes? What could it do for us when we begin slipping in either direction?

Meekness can temper our anger in a healthy way with reason. It can help us respond appropriately to a problem that is confronting us. It can help us recognize the difference between simply needing a good night's sleep (knowing things will look better in the morning) and needing to step up and deal with a situation or person. Meekness makes it possible for us to know when and how to make our "whip of cords" and which "tables to overturn."

Meekness reminds us we have the right, even the duty, to become angry at times, but never the license to let that anger explode uncontrolled.

But, then too, this virtue isn't about anger only. It's about love. Meekness helps us love those around us who really irritate us. And, it seems, someone always does. Sometimes we're able to avoid him or her. Sometimes we aren't. In either case, it's meekness that helps us come up with or recognize a solution. It's meekness that, as with Saint Thérèse, helps us see Christ in that person. Helps us love Christ more, love Christ better, by showing love to that person.

Not that it's easy. It doesn't happen without a lot of prayer and effort. And even then sometimes, as with Saint Thérèse, we need to admit to ourselves we've lost a particular battle in trying to be pleasant and hastily retreat. We need to admit to ourselves we have to regroup and muster our forces — our meekness — before the next meeting to allow that virtue to not only temper our anger but help us better see the world, the situation, through the eyes of the person who so tries our patience.

Thérèse, one of the most popular saints of the twentieth century, taught us that no matter where we go, no matter who we're with, there are people who, at times, will annoy us.

But it's important when thinking about meekness to remember that even when we're alone — even if we lived by ourselves with no contact with the outside world — there are times when we annoy *ourselves*. Who hasn't done something sinful and then been angry with himself or herself about that action, about that choice? Again, it's meekness that helps us confront ourselves. Helps us be honest in not only admitting but in evaluating our mistakes. Helps us forgive ourselves even as we seek God's forgiveness. Meekness helps us move on, to become wiser, stronger, holier.

But how do we increase our meekness? How do we better tap into this incredible resource that can change our daily lives? In a lot of ways any virtue is like a muscle. The more we use it, the stronger it becomes. (And then, when facing a situation where we *really* need it, it's there for us.)

One of the keys to meekness is our relationship with the Holy Spirit. The Church says the traditional fruits of the Spirit are charity, joy, peace, patience, kindness, goodness, generosity, gentleness, faithfulness, modesty, self-control, and chastity. (The gifts of the Spirit are wisdom, understanding, counsel, fortitude, knowledge, piety, and fear of the Lord.) The list is taken from Paul's letter to the Galatians (5:22–23). Here gentleness means meekness.

If we want to become "stronger at being meeker," we need to turn to the Holy Spirit because, as the *Catechism of the Catholic Church* reminds us, it's "by this power of the Spirit, God's children can bear much fruit."

We walk by the Spirit as we renounce—say no to—ourselves (Galatians 5:25). And when we do that, as we do that, we increase our inheritance, our ownership of the earth—of God's kingdom already here and, at the same time, yet to come. That's true because, to quote Saint Basil (who was Saint Gregory of Nyssa's older brother): "Through the Holy Spirit we are restored to paradise, led back to the kingdom of heaven."

Find our way home.

To read more about it

Anger, the Misunderstood Emotion by Carol Tavris (New York: Simon & Schuster, 1982)

Story of a Soul by Saint Thérèse of Lisieux, translated by John Clarke, O.C.D. (Washington, D.C.: ICS Publications, 1976)

Summa Theologica by Saint Thomas Aquinas (New York: Beniziger, 1946)

"Upon Our Lord's Sermon on the Mount," Sermon XXII, Discourse II, by John Wesley in *The Works of John Wesley* (Grand Rapids, Mich.: Zondervan, 1958)

Blessed are those who hunger and thirst for righteousness, for they will be filled

In Scripture

Jesus was talking to people who understood hunger. For them it wasn't a matter of deciding "I could go for a snack" in the middle of the afternoon and then rummaging through the kitchen cupboards, staring at shelves of food and complaining "There's nothing to eat in this house!"

No, these were people who earned a day's pay for a day's work. And if they didn't work one day, there was no income. There was no money for food. There was no meal. The family simply went without. And there was no guarantee of when its members would eat again. If tomorrow there was no work, then . . .

There were no food banks, no food stamps, no running up the charge card.

Then it would be another day of real hunger—not "Gee, it was so busy at work I didn't get lunch and I'm starving," and not "This twelve hundred-calories-a-day diet is killing me."

And the people understood thirst. For them there was no heading to the nearest drinking fountain, cracking open a fresh bottle of water, popping the top on a soft drink, grabbing another cup of coffee or—when "roughing it"—getting a glass of tap water.

These were folks who had learned to survive in a region where water was, and still is, scarce.

So when Jesus started talking about those who were hungry and thirsty his listeners knew what he meant. At times, they had experienced both hunger and thirst, and knew that they would again, as their people had in the past.

Their ancestors had headed for Egypt when famine ravaged their homeland. Generations later they had wandered in the desert on their return and were told God "humbled you by letting you hunger, then by feeding you with manna, with which neither you nor your ancestors were acquainted, in order to make you understand that one does not live by bread alone, but by every word that comes from the mouth of the Lord" (Deuteronomy 8:3).

On their journey God gave them "bread from heaven" in their hunger and "water . . . out of the rock" in their thirst (Nehemiah 9:15).

Book after book in the Old Testament tells of these people going hungry. In the good times they were reminded to not forget the bad (Sirach 18:25). They cried out in anguish as a lack of food decimated their number, not sparing even the most innocent among them—"Lift your hands to him for the lives of your children, who faint for hunger at the head of every street" (Lamentations 2:19). And at times they decided "happier were those pierced by the sword than those pierced by hunger, whose life drains away, deprived of the produce of the field" (Lamentations 4:9). Better a quick, bloody death than having to face what Ezekiel called "deadly arrows of famine" (Ezekiel 5:16).

And the ancestors of Jesus' followers suffered from thirst time and again, century after century. "The people thirsted there for water; and the people complained against Moses and said, 'Why did you bring us out of Egypt, to kill us and our children and livestock with thirst?'" (Exodus 17:3).

When an enemy cut off their community's supply of water in order to defeat them "their children were listless, and the women and young men fainted from thirst and were collapsing in the streets of the town and in the gateways; they no longer had any strength" (Judith 7:22).

The people listening to Jesus knew that even as they slept, hunger and thirst could torment them—"Just as when a hungry person dreams of eating and wakes up still hungry, or a thirsty person dreams of drinking and wakes up faint, still thirsty." (Isaiah 29:8).

They knew those who hunger and thirst are not passive; they seek out what they need.

They are like the deer that "yearns for flowing streams" (Psalms 42:1). A deer that is parched—any animal in the wild that needs water—doesn't simply sit there. It moves. It sniffs. It searches. It is active in the pursuit of its goal. It is unrelenting.

It's the difference between wishing something would happen and becoming consumed with the desire to have it happen. In our own time, the difference between talking about getting in shape and the day by day, step by step eating right and exercising that bring it about. The difference between simply wanting to quit smoking and going through the personal hell of becoming a nonsmoker.

"Ya gotta want it" is popular motivational sports phrase. Those who hunger and thirst want it.

Want what? Matthew's fourth Beatitude, like his first, has a softer spin on it than Luke's. Luke, the great lover of the poor, says "blessed are you who are hungry now, for you will be filled" (Luke 6:21). Matthew, in the same way he softened "poor" with "in spirit," has people hungry and thirsty "for righteousness."

Dikaiosune, the word Matthew uses that is translated as righteousness, means living in accordance with God's will. It can mean social justice. It can also mean love of God, demonstrated in our trust and obedience to him and our love of others in service and forgiveness. And it can mean our justification, the reestablishment of our right relationship with God.

There are some Scripture scholars who say righteousness in this particular Beatitude means God's saving activity.

Who in the Bible demonstrated righteousness? Abraham and Tobit are two examples from the Old Testament. Abraham showed righteousness by his faith (Genesis 15:6) and Tobit by his works of charity (Tobit 1:3). In the New Testament, Jesus singled out John the Baptist as a model of righteousness (Matthew 21:32).

"Strive first for the kingdom of God and his righteousness," Jesus told the people. Then "all these things"—something to eat and drink, something to wear, a place to live—"will be given to you as well" (Matthew 6:33). The righteous "do not worry about tomorrow"; they know "tomorrow will bring worries of its own" (Matthew 6:34).

But it is *God's* righteousness and not their own that they need. Jesus addressed the parable of the Pharisee and the tax collector coming to the temple to pray "to some who trusted in themselves that they were righteous and regarded others with contempt," (Luke 18:9–14). In his lesson, he taught "all who exalt themselves will be humbled, but all who humble themselves will be exalted."

And he promised in his fourth Beatitude that the people who go on the hunt for right eousness "will be filled." They will be satisfied. They will be belt-loosening, top-pants-button-unbuttoning full.

Chortazesthai had meant the fattening up of animals getting ready to be killed. When referring to humans, it had informally come to mean—to use our common phrase—stuffed. It was Jesus' guarantee if we hunger and thirst for doing God's will, we would be filled "up to here."

Down through the ages

Saint John Chrysostom (c. 347–407) was known for his brilliant preaching. He was good at talking and giving long sermons. How brilliant? *Chrysostom* means golden mouthed. How long? Up to two hours.

In a series of homilies on the Sermon on the Mount, Chrysostom rhetorically asked what Jesus meant when he used the term righteousness. "It's either the whole of virtue," virtue itself, he answered his own question, or "that particular virtue which is opposed to covetousness."

Covetousness? That may seem like a vice, a sin, we don't hear much about—or maybe even think much about—these days. There are commandments telling us to not covet our "neighbor's wife" or "goods" but what is covetousness and how is it the opposite of righteousness?

We use a couple of other words that mean the same thing—avarice, greed, the inordinate love of money, power, and fame. (Ah, yes. This sounds familiar.) Avarice is a "big time" sin, one of the seven "deadly" ones along with pride, lust, anger, gluttony, envy, and sloth; it's said they are the source of all the other sins.

Covetousness, Chrysostom taught, is the opposite of righteousness. And, he added, Jesus' use of it in the fourth Beatitude is pivotal because it leads into the fifth, which deals with showing mercy in order to be shown mercy.

"And see with what exceeding force he puts it," this Father of the Church stressed. "For he said not, 'Blessed are they which keep fast by righteousness' but, 'Blessed are they who do hunger and thirst after righteousness': that not haphazardly, but with all desire we may pursue it."

We can't go after it "haphazardly" or in any half-hearted way. And instead of desiring—craving, going after at all costs—money, power, and fame, we need to "transfer this desire to a new object, freedom from covetousness."

Righteousness has to become our goal.

Chrysostom goes on to explain that it is not covetousness or greed that makes one rich, but righteousness that brings true riches. It is the righteous, not the covetous, who "will be filled." "It is thought the rich are commonly made such by covetousness. . . . It is just the contrary; for it is righteousness that does this. Wherefore, so long as you act righteously, do not fear poverty, nor tremble at hunger. For the extortioners, they are the very persons who lose all, even as he certainly who is in love with righteousness possesses himself the good of all men in safety."

And if "they who covet not other men's goods enjoy so great abundance," then "much more [will] they who give up their own [goods]." The righteous person who gives away, who shares, what he or she has will be given even more in return.

Saint Catherine of Siena (1347–80) explained the relationship between righteousness, justice, and the correcting of those who are in sin. A member of the Dominican Laity, she's one of only two women named as doctors of the Church (the other is Saint Teresa of Avila). In her writing, Catherine used the first person to denote the voice of God speaking through her.

The Church's early leaders, she said, "offered me [that is, God] the just sacrifice of their holy and honorable lives. . . . With humility they trampled pride underfoot and like angels approached the table of the altar."

"Because they had first done justice to themselves," Catherine continued in God's voice, "they were just to their subjects as well. They wanted them to live virtuously, and so corrected them without any slavish fear, for their concern was not for themselves but only for my honor and the salvation of souls. . . . They corrected lovingly, with the ointment of kindness along with the harshness of the fire that cauterizes the wound of sin through reproof and penance, now more, now less, according to the gravity of the sin. Nor did it concern them that such correcting and speaking the truth might bring them death."

In contrast, Catherine stressed, in her own time there were religious and civil leaders who were *not* living—or seeking—a righteous life and so would "pretend not to see" what was happening.

"And do you know why?" she asked. "Because the root of selfish love is alive in them, and this is the source of their perverse slavish fear. They do not correct people for fear of losing their rank and position and their material possessions."

They remained silent because they were living a life of, to use Chrysostom's word, covetousness. Of avarice. Of greed.

These leaders "act as if they were blind, so they do not know how to maintain their position," Catherine scolded. "For if they saw how it is by holy justice that their positions are to be maintained, they would maintain them. . . . They believe they can succeed through injustice, by not reproving the sins of their subjects. But they are deceived by their own sensual passion, by their hankering for civil and ecclesiastical rank." These leaders didn't want to rock the boat for fear it would jeopardize their comfortable position.

Not one to back away from what she saw as the truth that needed to be told, Catherine added, "another reason they will not correct others is that they themselves are living in the same or greater sins."

Far from being hungry and thirsty for righteousness, these leaders were out to keep the money and power they had now, and even add to it. "Even what [wrongs and injustices] they do see," Catherine said, "they do not correct, but let themselves be won over by flattery and bribes, using these very things as excuses for not punishing the offenders."

They are, she said, the blind leading the blind (Matthew 15:14).

In stark contrast, the righteous — "those who have been or would be . . . gentle ministers" — "did not and would not act this way . . . because they follow the teaching of my Truth." Not "lukewarm," "they are ablaze in the furnace of my charity. They have no use for the world's honors and ranks and pleasures. Therefore, they are not afraid to correct. Those who do not hanker after power or ecclesiastical rank have no fear of losing it."

But speaking out as Catherine did, pushing to live a life of righteousness and create a society based on it, can take a toll. In our own time, Dr. Martin Luther King Jr. (1929–68) wrote about that high price. And about the incredible reward—the satisfaction—that can come with it.

In a sermon, the Baptist minister talked about the fear that gripped him as he and his family continued to get death threats while he was leading the Montgomery, Alabama, bus protest that began in 1955. After getting an anonymous threatening call in the middle of the night, he said, he got out of bed and began to pace the floor.

King went to the kitchen, made a pot of coffee, and admitted to himself "I was ready to give up." He "tried to think of a way to move out of the picture without appearing to be a coward." Then, "in this state of exhaustion, when my courage had almost gone, I determined to take my problem to God." He prayed out loud at the kitchen table, and years later the words were "still vivid in [his] memory": "'I am here taking a stand for what I believe is right. But now I am afraid. The people are looking for me for leadership, and if I stand before them without strength and courage, they too will falter. I am at the end of my powers. I have nothing left. I've come to the point where I can't face it alone.'"

It was then, King said, he experienced "the presence of the Divine as I had never experienced him." He could hear "the quiet assurance of an inner voice, saying, 'Stand up for righteousness, stand up for truth. God will be at your side.'"

His fears began to leave him. His uncertainty was gone. He felt ready to face anything. While his outer situation remained the same, "God had given me inner calm."

Three nights later, the family's home was bombed. King said he accepted the news without getting upset. His "experience with God" had given him "a new strength and trust." Now he knew "God is able to give us the interior resources to face the storms and problems of life."

He knew those who hunger and thirst for righteousness end up satisfied.

King returned to that theme in an article he wrote. He described how, following the search for justice, hungering for justice, we can find the peace of God. We can find spiritual fullness even in the middle of turmoil.

The civil rights leader said he had felt God's power changing "the fatigue of despair into the buoyancy of hope." And he had become convinced "the universe is under the control of a loving purpose, and that in the struggle for righteousness man has cosmic companionship."

We are never alone. Our God is always with us.

For us today

We've become a society big on goal setting. We admire those in business, in sports, in their personal and professional lives who can come up with a list of milestones they want to reach and then get there.

The seminar buzz phrase is "people don't plan to fail, they just fail to plan."

There's truth to that. If we have a plan, if we know our target, we can tell if we're getting closer to it, if we're remaining stagnant, if we're slipping farther from it. The process isn't complicated, successful people assure us. It's step by step. Day by day. But if it's easy, we can argue, why doesn't everyone succeed?

Ah, the goal-reachers answer, no one said it was *easy*. At times it's very hard. It's a million choices, a million decisions. It's taking that tiny step toward that huge goal again and again and again. No, it isn't easy. It's *simple*. There's a difference. Attempting to reach a goal can be hard without being complicated.

And that, in a nutshell, is the Christian lifestyle. That, in a nutshell, is hungering and thirsting for righteousness.

It's simple, but far from easy.

How simple? Love God. Love your neighbor as you love yourself.

How far from easy? So far that even when we begin to get a glimmer of understanding, of personal awareness, that this is what we *really* want, *really* need to make our lives as complete as they can possibly be on earth, we close our eyes to it. We turn our backs on it. We run in the opposite direction.

And when we do that, not surprisingly, it becomes harder to see that true goal. That goal which is truth. Harder to take the steps that will bring us closer to it. Harder to live a closer-to-Christian lifestyle day by day. Harder to make the right—the righteous—decisions as we face all the choices that crowd our lives.

How can we get back on track? How can we begin to see our true goal more clearly? How can we even recognize it as our true goal? As *the* true goal? By humbly turning to God. By asking for his help. By prayer. By fasting. By taking advantage of the sacrament of reconciliation. By receiving the Eucharist.

That all sounds so . . . if not medieval, at least conservative. After all, we don't want to become "right-wing religious fanatics"—a group "known" for its hypocrisy and narrow-mindedness if not racism and thinly veiled greed.

So again, how can we get back on track? How can we begin to see our true goal more clearly? How ever recognize it as our true goal? As *the* true goal? The answer is by humbly serving our God in our fellow human beings. By not just being concerned for those around us but by becoming staunch supporters of the laws, the programs, the agencies, the organizations that help and protect the needy and vulnerable in our society. That give them not just a handout but a hand up. That take care of their immediate critical needs and promote their future ability to take care of themselves. That help them get food, housing, education, and jobs.

That all sounds so . . . if not communist, at least liberal. After all, we don't want to become "left-wing socialist zealots"—a group "known" for its hypocrisy and narrow-mindedness if not finger-pointing and not-so-thinly veiled godlessness.

And we can't be both, can we? Certainly not at the same time.

We can be. We're called to be. Not "conservative fanatics" or "liberal zealots" but imitators of Jesus, the righteous one. Jesus, who spent so many nights alone in prayer to his heavenly Father. Jesus, who loved and helped others even to the point of scandalizing some people by healing on the Sabbath. Jesus, who loved God and his neighbor as himself. Like Jesus, we are to be signs of contradiction—"a sign that will be opposed" within our own culture (Luke 2:34).

Even in our own era those who choose to live righteously confuse the rest of us. Dorothy Day, cofounder of the Catholic Worker Movement, was notorious for her outspoken views and actions against war and nuclear weapons. She was also known for her solid Catholic personal beliefs and personal foundation (rosary, encyclicals, confessor).

In the same way, readers of *Journal of a Soul,* the autobiography of Pope John XXIII, are amazed the pontiff credited with throwing open the windows of the Church some four centuries after the Council of Trent was also a person who fostered and maintained a private prayer life that was so traditional if not downright rigid.

We find the truly righteous hard to understand because so often we see only half of the problem or half of the solution. But there can be no halves. There is only a whole.

No wonder someone singing the praises of only a part of righteousness is an easy target for critics. (The politician who makes a show of his "Christianity" but votes only for military or big business and never for social service. The social activist who harps on respect and tolerance for diversity but slams anyone who utters a traditional Christian belief.) The split—the inconsistency, the dichotomy, the gaping chasm—is clear in so many areas. Take the pro-life/pro-choice (anti-choice/pro-abortion) debate for example.

Who's the conservative and who's the liberal?

—"We support a woman's right to choose to have an abortion under any circumstances but oppose capital punishment."

—"We support the state's right to impose the death penalty but oppose abortion."

Those emotion-packed issues can become even more intense when they affect us personally. When it's someone we love who is facing an unwanted, an ill-timed, or a medically threatening pregnancy. When it's someone we love who has been murdered or is facing a state-sanctioned death for committing a murder.

It shouldn't surprise us that there can be a lot of discomfort involved in seeking righteousness. Jesus is telling us there can be a devastating hunger, an almost all-consuming thirst, as we try first to discover and then to live God's will for us.

God's will for each of us.

What does it mean for *me* to hunger and thirst for righteousness? It means I am obligated to examine the unique gifts and talents an all-loving God has given me. It means I am obligated to face the hardships and heartaches that are a part of my life here on earth.

As a Christian, as a human being, I am called upon to develop my talents. To use my gifts in service to others, in praise to God. But I can't be smug because I'm more talented in some areas than the people around me are. And I can't despair because those around me are more talented in other areas.

Just as in Jesus' parable about the rich man and the three servants (Matthew 25:14–30), God has given some of us five talents, some of us two, and some of us only one. He asks only that we use what we have and that we not bury our gifts. If I have five talents, I should use all five; if I have two, I should use both; if I have only one, I should use that one.

And if we do that and if we keep our eyes on the big picture, as Jesus promises in this Beatitude, the little details will take care of themselves. Then we won't worry so much about what we will eat, where we will sleep, what we will wear. God will give us all that. But those aren't the things that will make us satisfied. No, the deeper hunger and thirst we feel—the hunger and thirst for our God—will begin to ease.

Day by day, step by step, choice by choice, God will continue to fill us more and more with his love.

To read more about it

The Dialog by Saint Catherine of Siena, translated by Susanne Noffke, O.P. (New York: Paulist Press, 1980)

Dorothy Day: A Biography by William D. Miller (San Francisco: Harper & Row, 1982)

Journal of a Soul by Pope John XXIII (New York: McGraw Hill, 1965)

The Preaching of Chrysostom edited by Jaroslav Pelikan (Philadelphia: Fortress, 1967)

Spirituality of the Beatitudes: Matthew's Challenge for First World Christians by Michael H. Crosby, O.F.M. Cap. (Maryknoll, N.Y.: Orbis, 1981)

Blessed are the merciful, for they will receive mercy

In Scripture

Sometimes when the same word is repeated again and again we stop hearing it. That can be the case with *mercy*. In English versions of the Bible it appears almost two hundred times. Originally, in the Old Testament the Hebrew *hesed* (or *chesed*) was used. In the New, it was the Greek *eleos*.

What do these words mean? Scripture scholars aren't in agreement on how to translate them, but they are certain our word *mercy* is much too limited. *Hesed* was more than simply compassion shown to someone who was in need of forgiveness. It was basic to the Jewish religion and morality. It was intimately linked with Yahweh's plan of salvation and the covenant between God and his chosen people, and with righteousness and justice.

It was a word used frequently when describing God or how God acts.

In Genesis, when angels were urging Lot to leave the soon-to-be-destroyed town of Sodom, he hesitated. Then they "seized him and his wife and his two daughters by the hand, the Lord being merciful to him, and they brought him out and left him outside the city" (Genesis 19:16).

In Exodus, after the Egyptian troops were destroyed in the Red Sea, Moses and the Israelites sang a song to the Lord that included the line "in your steadfast love [or mercy] you led the people whom you redeemed; you guided them by your strength to your holy abode" (Exodus 15:13).

God's mercy seems very concrete. It's grabbing a good person by the hand and leading him or her away from danger (away from sin and the consequences of that sin). It's leading them—after they have listened to God and agreed to follow—out of their misery. It's redeeming them, saving them from that misery and from that hopelessness. And it's guiding them to a place that is God's—a holy dwelling that in our own time we might consider not a place but a state of being. Because of God's mercy, it's possible for us to draw closer to him, to love him and feel his love more fully, right here, right now.

Later in Exodus, after giving Moses the Ten Commandments, Yahweh promised to bestow "steadfast love [or again, mercy] to the thousandth generation of those who love me and keep my commandments" (Exodus 20:6). (In the previous verse, he had already threatened to punish only to the "third and fourth generation" the children of those who were wicked.) God will pour out his mercy not only on the person who is righteous (who lives his commandments) but also on that person's children and grandchildren. Generation after generation will reap the benefits of that person's faithfulness to the Lord.

The Israelites knew—and were reminded when they forgot—God's mercy was an integral part of their history, of their coming to and surviving in the Promised Land. "I will declare to you all the saving deeds of the Lord performed for you and for your ancestors," Samuel told the people (1 Samuel 12:7).

And, the people knew, God's mercy could be depended upon, unlike their fellow humans'. "I am in great distress," David said. "Let me fall into the hand of the Lord, for his mercy is very great; but let me not fall into human hands" (1 Chronicles 21:13).

God's mercy was considered eternal. It "endures forever" (2 Chronicles 7:3). If you have sinned, the "gracious and merciful" Lord "will not turn away his face from you if you return to him" (2 Chronicles 30:9). And that guarantee was a part of the contract—the deal—the Israelites had with Yahweh, a covenant of mercy with "those who love him and keep his commandments" (Nehemiah 1:5).

Not that they could simply do as they pleased and expect God's mercy, a kind of "get-out-of-jail-free card" they could play at any time. But if they confessed their wrongdoing and returned to God, he would forgive them, accept them back and pour his blessings on them.

"Have mercy on me, O God, according to your steadfast love; according to your abundant mercy blot out my transgressions" (Psalm 51:3).

The Israelites knew confessing their mistakes was the key to redemption. "No one who conceals transgressions will prosper, but one who confesses and forsakes them will obtain mercy" (Proverbs 28:13).

But it wasn't quite that simple. To return to God, to live the commandments and become righteous involved a specific act or attitude that influenced the receiving of God's mercy. One had to show it, had to give it, to get it.

Jesus is simply repeating that promise in his fifth Beatitude. Mercy—the blessing of being led by the hand from evil and hopelessness—is something we all want. But if we want to be forgiven and to be shown compassion, we must forgive, and we must be compassionate.

That's so central to Christ's message he included it in the prayer he taught his apostles. They knew Jesus was a person of prayer, one who drew strength from spending time alone talking to and listening to his heavenly Father. Teach us how to pray, they asked. How do you do it? What do you say?

He taught them the Lord's Prayer. He gave them (and us) the line we now say as "forgive us our trespasses as we forgive those who trespass against us." (In Matthew 6:12, it's "debts" and "debtors," and in Luke 11:4, it's "and forgive us our sins for we forgive everyone indebted to us.")

Forgive us as much as we forgive others.

It was Peter—brash, talk-first and think-later Peter—who asked Jesus just how many times he and the others were expected to forgive someone (Matthew 18:21-35). "Seven?" he asked, meaning a bunch. No, Jesus replied, "seventy-seven," meaning an infinite number. Jesus then goes on to tell the parable of the servant who was forgiven a huge debt by a king but refused to erase the small debt that was owed him by a fellow servant. The king heard of it and "in anger . . . handed him over to be tortured until he would pay his entire debt."

"So my heavenly Father will also do to everyone of you, if you do not forgive your brother and sister from your heart," Jesus concluded.

To receive mercy we must imitate our merciful God because "with the judgment you make you will be judged, and the measure you give will be the measure you get" (Matthew 7:2). If we're stingy with our mercy to those around us, we can expect the same from God. We're promised the same. "If you forgive others their trespasses, your heavenly Father will also forgive you; but if you do not forgive others, neither will your Father forgive your trespasses" (Matthew 6:14).

If we don't show mercy (*hesed, eleos*) to the people around us, we can't expect to receive it. To be led by the hand from evil. To be brought to a holy place. To be warmly welcomed back when we admit our faults to God. To be a part of a covenant between God and humans that stretches back "a thousand generations."

No, "judgment will be without mercy to anyone who has shown no mercy; mercy triumphs over judgment" (James 2:13). No, it is the merciful who will be shown mercy.

Down through the ages

Saint Caesarius of Arles was a reluctant bishop; he didn't want the job in sixth-century Gaul. Known and loved for his holiness and kindness, he headed his see for four decades.

"The idea of mercy is sweet," he said, "but how much sweeter is mercy itself?"

Mercy, he noted in a sermon, "is what all wish to receive, but few are willing to give." But, he questioned, "how can you seek what you refuse to give?" If a person expects to receive mercy in heaven, the bishop said, he or she better be giving it here on earth.

"Since we all desire mercy," he went on, "let us make mercy our patroness in this world so that she may free us in the world to come. For there is mercy in heaven, but it is attained through earthly paths of mercy."

Inch by inch, or stone by stone, we create our pathway to God's mercy, to our eternal happiness.

This means, Caesarius said, there's earthly and heavenly mercy, human and divine mercy. The difference is "human mercy regards the miseries of the poor" while "divine mercy grants forgiveness of sins."

"Whatever human mercy provides here on earth," he continued, "divine mercy will return to us in heaven. In the poor of this world, God is left neglected and hungry. For as Jesus once said, What you did to the least of my brothers you did to me. Indeed, God who sees fit to give his mercy in heaven wishes to receive mercy here on earth."

"What sort of people are we?" the bishop asked. "When God gives, we want to receive, but when he begs, we do not want to give."

He then reminded his listeners that when the poor are hungry, it is Christ who is in need. "As Christ said, I was hungry and you gave me nothing to eat (Matthew 25:42). Do not despise the misery of the poor, if you wish to ensure the forgiveness of your sins. Christ hungers now, my brothers and sisters. In all who are poor he himself deigns to hunger and thirst. And what he will later give in heaven is the same as what he now receives on earth."

We're going to get what we give.

"What do you wish for, what do you seek, my friends, when you come to church?" he asked the people. "What, if not mercy? So show mercy on earth, and that you may receive it in heaven."

It's not complicated, he explained. "A poor person asks you for something; you ask God for something. He begs for a mouthful of food; you beg for eternal life.

"Give to the one who begs that you may be worthy to receive from Christ," he said. "Listen to Christ's words: Give and it will be given to you. I cannot understand how you have the nerve to ask for what you refuse to give. . . . So give to the poor according to your means."

A thousand years later in that same part of the world, another French cleric was delivering—and living—the same message. Saint Vincent de Paul (c. 1580–1660) would later be declared the patron of all charitable groups (including the one bearing his name, the Saint Vincent de Paul Society, founded in 1833 by a young French layman, Frederic Ozanam).

Vincent de Paul was no stranger to harsh conditions. When he was twenty-five he was captured by pirates and sold as a slave in Algeria but was able to escape after two years. As a priest his work included ministering to galley slaves as well as the poor whom he knew so well and loved so deeply.

"Although poor people are sometimes unpolished and ill-mannered," he wrote, "we should not judge them by appearances or by their intellectual abilities. But if you regard the poor with the eyes of faith, you will see that they take the place of the Son of God who chose to be poor."

Jesus' "mission was to preach to the poor," Vincent said. "We should have the same spirit and follow Christ's example, that is, we must care for the poor, comfort them, help them, and support them."

"Christ wanted to be poor," the priest noted. "He called disciples who were poor" and "became the servant of the poor and . . . shared in their poverty." Much more than that, Jesus even said that he "would count every act that helps or hurts the poor as done for or against himself."

"As God loves the poor, he also loves those who love the poor," Vincent said. Why would that be so? "If one person loves another, he also loves anyone who loves or serves the one he loves."

That's why "we hope that God will love us for the sake of the poor."

That's why "we try to be compassionate when we visit the poor."

Why "we identify with them so fully that we can say with Paul: I have become all things to all men" (1 Corinthians 9:22).

That's the reason, Vincent said, "we should be moved by our neighbors' troubles and concerns" and "should ask God to fill our hearts with feelings of mercy and compassion and to continue to fill them with these dispositions."

And our love and action can't be low on our to-do list, he stressed. "We should prefer the service of the poor to everything else and render this service as soon as possible," he said.

As the founder of an order of priests and cofounder of an order of sisters, Vincent de Paul wrote about following rules, but he made it clear that "if a poor person needs medicine or other help during the time of prayer, do what needs to be done with peace of mind. Offer the action to God as your prayer.

"Do not be uneasy or feel guilty because you interrupted your prayer to serve the poor," he taught. "You do not neglect God if you leave him for such service. You are merely interrupting one service of God to carry out another. So when you postpone your prayer to serve some poor person, remember that this very service is done for God. For charity is more important than any rule.

"Moreover," he continued, "all rules must lead to charity. She is a noble mistress, and we must do whatever she commands. With new zeal we must serve the poor, especially the oppressed and indigent. They are given to us as our masters and benefactors."

In our own time, a sister has become world renowned for her love of the poor, "especially outcasts and beggars"—the poorest of the poor.

Mother Teresa of Calcutta noted, "Now, more than ever we need to live out the teaching of Jesus: 'Love one another as the Father has loved Me' [John 15:9, 12]."

What we are asked to do—what is demanded of us, she said, is to "love as the Father loves his Son Jesus, with the same mercy and compassion, joy and peace." We need to "find out how the Father loves his Son, and then try to love one another in the same way."

Find out how much Jesus loves you, she continued. And then love in the same way.

In each person's life, Mother Teresa said, "Jesus comes as the Bread of Life—to be eaten, to be consumed by us. That is how he loves us. He also comes as the Hungry One, hoping to be fed with the bread of our life, with our hearts that love and our hands that serve."

By doing that, "we prove that we have been created in the image and likeness of God, for God is love."

"When we love we are like God," she said. "This is what Jesus meant when he said: Be perfect as your heavenly Father is perfect."

Echoing the words of Christ, of Caesarius, and of Vincent de Paul, Mother Teresa taught, "As you love God, you must love the poor: in their suffering."

And our love of the poor, she said, "overflows" from our love for God.

"You must find the poor and serve them," she explained. "When you have found them, you must take them to your heart. We owe our people [the poor] the greatest gratitude because they allow us to touch Christ."

For us today

It's tempting to believe that our baptism means we no longer have to fly coach. If all the people of the world are on a jumbo jet heading for the end of time, those of us who follow Christ have been bumped up to first class.

With this Beatitude, Jesus says that isn't so. No, being a Catholic, being a Christian means we can't sit back and wait for our drink and meal to be delivered to us. It means we're the ones who are working. We're the flight attendants who have to not only answer when someone hits his or her call light, but we have to continuously walk the aisles recognizing or even anticipating passengers' needs and then attempt to meet those needs.

In the same way, being a Catholic, being a Christian, doesn't mean sitting at the head banquet table. It means tying on an apron. Grabbing a tray for bussing tables. Picking up a scrub brush for scouring the pots and pans.

Jesus was very clear on this. And his example did not just confuse his apostles, it startled them. Here, let me show you, he said on the night before he died. He got up from the table and began to wash their feet. "You do not know now what I am doing, but later you will understand," he said (John 13:7).

You say I'm the master and the teacher, Jesus told them, and you should. I am. So if I do this then . . . ?

Then they should do this. Then we should do this.

This is a part of mercy—a part of loving others, a part of loving Christ by loving others, a part of the new covenant we have inherited. We ask for God's mercy; we must show others mercy.

We must feed the hungry, clothe the naked, welcome the stranger—and fulfill all those other commands that are so familiar from the parable on the Last Judgment (Matthew 25:31–46). But one of the problems we face in doing that, one of the excuses we rely on so heavily and dearly love, is the one argued by those in the parable who *didn't* do those things, and so didn't show their love of God by loving others. And, at the same time, it's the puzzling question posed by those who *did* do those things, and so did show their love of God by loving others.

"When did we see you?" members of both groups want to know.

So even those who did what God asks didn't always see Christ in the ones they were serving. And those who didn't do what God asks— apparently they never saw him. But, it seems safe to say, they never looked very hard either.

Mother Teresa says we have to keep looking. We have to "find the poor." We can't be content with some abstract or contradictory notion of mercy. The old "I love all humanity, it's just people I can't stand" cannot guide our actions. It's in people—in individuals—that we will discover Christ *as we serve them.*

Or maybe, sometimes we won't. It seems safe to say that there will be times when those who love and serve the poor for Christ's sake *don't* see Jesus behind the dirty hands, the wrinkled face, the matted hair.

But those who want to receive God's mercy, those who realize how much they depend on God's mercy, continue to serve anyway. They serve when they are tired and when it's inconvenient. They serve when the ones they are helping are more than just ungrateful, but are resentful or belligerent, angry, hostile, self-centered, greedy, or smelly.

There are no violins playing softly in the background when we serve others. No hint of roses. There can be the harsh and unmistakable clanking of iron-barred doors slamming shut or the stench of urine-stained pants.

All that and more makes it easy to believe showing mercy has to do with going "out there," and it does—going to the county jail, going to the local shelter for the homeless, and so on. But it isn't, it can't be, limited to that.

We can go and serve—if not see—Christ there, but most of us don't live there. Our volunteer hours don't make up most of our day. They may be only a small fraction of our week or our month.

No, we also have to find Jesus in our everyday lives. In our home. In our neighborhood. In our parish, our school, our work place. In our families and in our friends. In those we naturally and easily love and in those—as with the nun in Saint Thérèse's convent—who set our teeth on edge.

Just as our religion, our beliefs, can't be "one hour of church on Sunday morning," they can't be two hours of volunteer work every other Friday or once a month either. Yes, there's no doubt we need that time of community worship on Sunday and we need to be of service every other week or every month, but day by day is how we live. Day by day is how God calls us to love.

We all know it's easier to be pleasant with the impatient woman in the food bank line than the jerk at the office. It's easier to imagine Christ in the grump as we hand him a bag of apples, macaroni and cheese, and bread, than to even think of Jesus as the boss who doesn't carry his share of the load at work and drones on and on at staff meetings, apparently in love with the sound of his own voice.

It's easier to think of the Church's traditional corporal works of mercy and spiritual works of mercy as "out there," not right here. Not right now. The corporal works of mercy are to feed the hungry, give drink to the thirsty, clothe the naked, shelter the homeless, help the sick, visit the imprisoned, and bury the dead. The spiritual works of mercy are to instruct the ignorant, correct sinners, advise the doubtful, show patience to sinners and those in error, forgive others, comfort the afflicted, and pray for the living and the dead.

Sometimes, just as the people in Jesus' parable didn't realize they were serving him by serving others, we can lose sight of the fact that we *are* serving others. We *are* doing those acts of mercy.

When we fix dinner for our family. When we give our young child the glass of water she's asking for. When we do those loads of laundry. When we take the time to show the new guy at work how to use the photocopy machine. When we make the effort to have lunch with a co-worker who wants help sorting out a personal problem. When we send a letter to or phone an elderly homebound relative. When we cover for a co-worker who's out with the flu. When we do these things we are serving others and performing those acts of mercy. We are serving Christ.

The opportunities are there. Often the tasks aren't complicated. Making brownies for a funeral luncheon at the parish. Staying out in the cold an extra ten or fifteen minutes to shovel the snow from a neighbor's front walk. Accepting a spouse's apology without tossing back an "I told you so."

It's when we reach out our hand to help someone else that God takes us by the hand, just as his angels did with Lot, and leads us away from evil. Away from temptation. Away from our weaknesses. It's then that, in his mercy, he leads us toward a "holy abode," leads us further into his kingdom.

To read more about it

God's Incredible Mercy by George A. Maloney, S.J. (New York: Alba House, 1989)

Mother Teresa: Contemplative in the Heart of the World by Mother Teresa (Ann Arbor, Mich.: Servant Publications, 1985)

The Principle of Mercy: Taking the Crucified People from the Cross by Jon Sobrino, S.J. (Maryknoll, N.Y.: Orbis, 1994)

With All Our Heart and Mind: The Spiritual Works of Mercy in a Psychological Age by Sidney Cornelia Callahan (New York: Crossroad, 1988)

Blessed are the pure in heart, for they will see God

In Scripture

Purity and cleanliness were important to the Hebrews. The Greek word for clean, *katharos*, can be found in the Old Testament more than one hundred and fifty times.

In general, *katharos* fell into one of four categories.

The first had to do with food. "Clean" animals could be eaten. "Unclean" couldn't. In the second chapter of Leviticus, the Lord explained the rules to Moses and Aaron. (The same material is reviewed in the fourteenth chapter of Deuteronomy.) A clean animal was defined as one that chewed its cud and had a cloven, or divided hoof. A cow was OK. A pig was not.

Why? Scripture scholars say the distinctions were made based on the customary ideas of hygiene, but here the acceptable and the unacceptable foods were now given moral or religious connotations. The Chosen People were not to eat anything unclean because they were called to be pure, to be dedicated to Yahweh.

Orthodox Jews still follow strict dietary laws. This is called "keeping kosher." Kosher refers to an adherence to those laws or it refers to an item prepared in accordance with them. The word itself is Yiddish, coming from the Hebrew *kasher* which means proper. Most of us are familiar with the "no pork" rule, but the pig wasn't the only animal specifically mentioned in Leviticus. The camel, the hare, and the rock badger were also forbidden. And it wasn't just that they couldn't eat any one of those, they couldn't even touch its dead carcass.

The division of clean and unclean applied to water animals, too. Proper food had fins and scales. Improper did not. A perch, for example, was considered acceptable, but an eel was not.

Reptiles were unclean and so was every animal that had been killed by another animal or died of natural causes. In general, birds of prey were also considered unclean.

Even insects were included on the list. The only clean ones were those with jointed legs, such as the grasshopper and locust.

The second general area of clean and unclean was concerned with leprosy. That term was used to describe a number of skin diseases, not just what we now call Hansen's disease. Chapters 13 and 14 of Leviticus contain details on how someone with a skin disease was to be brought to the priest for examination. He could declare the patient clean or unclean. If unclean, the person had to wear torn garments, keep his or her hair messy, and, if a man, cover his beard. The leper had to live outside the community and yell "Unclean" to anyone who might be coming near. If the disease went away, the leper had to go back to the priest who would declare him or her cured.

The third area of cleanliness had to do with death. Having contact with a dead body made a person unclean for seven days (Numbers 19:12, 14, 16). It wasn't just touching a body that made a person unclean, but even being in a tent with someone as he or she died or entering it after the death.

And the fourth area was concerned with sex. One became unclean with almost any sexual act or function, whether it was lawful or unlawful, or considered normal or abnormal. Again, the regulations can be found in the book of Leviticus.

One who was clean could take part in the cult or religious practices of the people. One who was unclean couldn't. Typically a person would become clean again after a period of time had passed and he or she had bathed. Uncleanliness, then, was more a physical than moral state.

In Jesus' time the Pharisees interpreted the laws of cleanliness and uncleanliness and they were known for their strictness. Their black-or-white attitude was one that brought sharp criticism from him. He called them "hypocrites" because they would "clean the outside of the cup and of the plate, but inside they are full of greed and self-indulgence" (Matthew 23:25). Jesus also upset the Pharisees and the scribes by allowing his disciples to ignore some of the traditional laws of cleanliness.

"Listen and understand," he explained, "it is not what goes into the mouth that defiles a person, but it is what comes out of the mouth that defiles" (Matthew 15:10–11).

With this Beatitude, Jesus wasn't concerned with cloven hoofs or skin diseases, with being near a dead person or with external rituals. He was talking about having a heart that shuns immorality, that chooses cleanliness, that is pure.

The heart is mentioned throughout the Bible. The people didn't understand its function in circulating oxygen-rich blood, but it was seen as the center of emotions. It could be cheerful, it could exult, it could be made merry with wine. It felt grief, impatience, worry, and hatred. A strong heart was a sign of courage, and it was the seat of intelligence.

The writers of Scripture used the word *heart* where we today would use *mind* or *will*. It was the source of an individual's thoughts, desires, and actions. To be "hard of heart" was to be stubborn, or to be slow to believe in Jesus.

A person was whatever his or her heart was, and only Yahweh could truly know one's heart.

The ones who have "clean hands and pure hearts" will "ascend the hill of the Lord," the psalmist said (Psalm 24:3–5). And will "receive blessing from the Lord." Later the writer added, "Truly God is good to the upright, to those who are pure of heart" (Psalm 73:1). Jesus said they were the ones who would "see God."

While Psalm 24 referred to taking part in temple worship, Jesus meant more than that.

To "come and behold the face of God" was a Hebrew idiom for visiting the temple (Psalm 42:2). No, Jesus meant the person who was pure of heart would see God in the coming kingdom.

Seeing God was what Moses had prayed for: "Show me your glory" (Exodus 33:18). It was what the psalmist had longed for: "As for me, I shall behold your face in righteousness; when I awake, I shall be satisfied, beholding your likeness" (Psalm 17:15). It was the promise made to the upright, those who would "live in your presence" (Psalm 140:13).

They would receive what we now call the beatific vision — the clear and full knowledge of God and God's love. They would see and love God as he sees and loves himself.

"Now we see in a mirror, dimly," Paul wrote, referring to the poor reflectors of his day, "but then we will see face to face" (1 Corinthians 13:12).

"When he [the risen and transfigured Jesus] is revealed," John explained, "we will be like him, for we will see him as he is. And all who have this hope in him purify themselves, just as he is pure" (1 John 3:2–3).

They strive to conform their thoughts, desires, and actions to God's will — they push themselves to become "pure of heart" — so that

they can become more like him, can one day
see him and love him face to face.

Down through the ages

John Cassian (360–435) described a couple of
concrete images to explain the relationship
between purity of heart and seeing God. In one
description he talked about a tower; in another,
a feather.

Cassian was known for the conferences,
the talks, he gave to his fellow monks. A fol-
lower of Saint John Chrysostom, he's considered a saint in the Eastern Church but was
never canonized in the West.

Cassian believed every monk who is looking
for "the perfect way . . . aims at uninterrupted
prayerfulness. As far as is possible to a frail man,
he struggles for imperturbable peace and purity
of mind."

That purity is essential to prayer, he taught,
and praying is our way of seeing God both now
and in the kingdom to come. "The keystone in
the arch of all virtues is perfect prayer," he
wrote, "and without this keystone the archway
become rickety and insecure."

But how does a person avoid the sin that
keeps him or her from leading a virtuous life
and, in doing so, keeps him or her from prayer?

It's impossible to become a person of prayer—to "build a tower"—"unless the ground is cleared of rotten or dead rubbish and the foundations are built on firm . . . soil or on rock," Cassian wrote. "So it is in the realm of the spirit. To build a tower of the spirit, you must clear the soul of its sins and passions and build firm foundations of simplicity and humility upon the Gospel: this is the only way the tower can rise unshakable, as high as heaven."

If we do that, he said, it will stand undamaged even as the "tempests of passion be poured upon it," "the floods of persecution beat upon it like battering-rams" and "the storm of hostile spirits blows upon it."

But how do we clear that ground and establish that foundation? "No one can offer prayer of proper intensity and sincerity, unless he is seeking to live thus," he said. "First, there must be no anxiety about the bodily needs—not to worry about a piece of business, but not even the recollection of it; no detraction; no gossip; above all, no anger nor wrongful sorrow, for these cannot but disturb the spirit; no lust of the flesh; no love of money.

"By clearing the ground—weeding out these and other public sins—a man makes his life pure, and attains the state of simplicity and innocence. Then he must lay a foundation deep enough to support a tower that will reach to heaven; and the only foundation deep and strong enough is humility."

Then, too, Cassian taught, to be pure of heart is to be like a clean feather.

"There is a good comparison between the soul and a delicate little feather," he wrote. "If a feather has not been touched by damp, it is so light that even the slightest breath of wind can puff it high into the air."

But if "even a little damp has weighed it down, it cannot float, and falls straight to the ground."

It's the same with our mind, the monk said. If it's not "burdened by sin and the cares of daily life and evil passion," it "has a natural purity which lifts it from the earth to heaven at the least breath of a meditation upon the invisible things of the spirit."

Jesus talked about this, Cassian taught, when he gave warning to "'Take heed that your hearts are not weighed down by surfeiting and drunkenness and the cares of the world'" (Luke 2:34).

"So if we want our prayers to reach the sky and beyond the sky," Cassian said, "we must make sure that the mind is so unburdened by the weights of sin and passion as to be restored to it natural buoyancy. Then the prayer will rise to God."

That's so, he continued, because "by purity of heart . . . the mind is abstracted from earthly feelings and is re-formed in the likeness of an angelic spirit. Then, whatever thought the mind receives, whatever it considers, whatever it does, will be a prayer of true purity and sincerity."

Saint Anthony of Padua (1195–1231) agreed. The Franciscan preacher pointed out the relationship between what Christ promised in the Sermon on the Mount and what he said during his Passion.

"The life of Christ always mirrored his teaching," Saint Anthony wrote, "as is evident from a concordance [agreement] of his teaching on the Mount of Beatitudes and their fulfillment on Calvary."

This sixth Beatitude parallels Christ's statement "Now it is finished" (John 19:30), Saint Anthony said. Why? Because "he who wishes to see God must put an end to sin, using the words of Christ on the cross: 'It is finished.'"

Seeing God comes from having a clean heart. A clean heart comes from saying good-bye to sin—saying "Enough!" "No more!" "That's all!"

St. Anthony also wrote about seeing God, seeing the face of Christ. We can't do that, he said, without first accepting his suffering.

"Blessed are the eyes of the pure of heart," the theologian wrote, "since they see God. Together with Job, they can say: 'Now my eye has seen you' (Job 42:5). Blessed indeed are those whose eyes have not been blinded by filthy lucre, not clouded by mundane concerns and solicitude. They are the ones who are able to perceive God wrapped in swaddling clothes, placed in a manger, and fleeing into Egypt. They are the ones who see God sitting on a donkey and hanging naked on the cross of shame. This is how the apostles saw Christ. Eyes afflicted with blindness, however, cannot see in this manner."

The Jesus that the pure of heart see, Saint Anthony wrote, is not one of only majesty and glory. They see a Jesus who "made for himself a tunic of the sackcloth of our human nature, sewing it with the needle of the subtle workings of the Holy Spirit and the thread of the faith of the Blessed Virgin."

But even more than that, the Franciscan stressed, Jesus "donned it, and embellished it with the dust of lowliness and poverty. Eyes afflicted with blindness cannot perceive this."

"'I say that many prophets and kings wished to see,'" Saint Anthony, quoting Christ (Matthew 13:17) and then explained, "The prophets are the corrupt leaders of the Church, and the kings are the powerful men of this earth. Both wish to see Christ in heaven, yet refuse to see him nailed to the shameful cross.

"They wish to reign with Christ," he continued, "but at the same time they want to enjoy themselves on this earth, hoping with [the Old Testament seer] Balaam: 'May I die the death of the just' (Numbers 23:10). They desire to see the glory of Christ's divinity which the apostles witnessed, without suffering the shame of the passion or the poverty of Christ which the apostles experienced."

That's why these leaders don't see Jesus as the apostles did, Saint Anthony said, but rather "with the wicked they will look 'on him whom they have pierced' (John 19:37). They will not hear the consoling words: 'Come, you have my Father's blessing'; instead they will hear the voice thunder: 'Out of my sight, you condemned'" (Matthew 25:34, 41).

No, he emphasized, "blessed are the eyes that see in the face of Jesus the bitterness of his passion, swollen with bruises and tears, smeared with spittle, because one day they will see that same face 'at which the angels love to look'" (1 Peter 1:12).

In more recent times the Danish philosopher and religious thinker Søren Kierkegaard (1813–55) wrote "purity of heart is to will one thing."

"We base our meditation on the Apostle James' words in his Epistle, chapter 4, verse 8," he said, "'Draw nigh to God and he will draw nigh to you. Cleanse your hands, ye sinners; and purify your hearts, ye double-minded.' For only the pure in heart can see God, and therefore draw nigh to Him; and only by God drawing nigh to them can they maintain this purity. And he who in truth wills only one thing can will only the Good, and he who only wills one thing when he wills the Good can only will the Good in truth."

In other words, to seek anything other than God—other than the Good—is to be "double-minded" because God is the only "single" goal there is.

"Let your heart in truth will only one thing," Kierkegaard said, "for therein is the heart's purity." And "purity of heart is the very wisdom that is acquired through prayer."

We may at times believe something other than God, other than the Good, can be a single goal, the philosopher said, but we're wrong. "The worldly goal is not one thing in its essence," he continued, but it can seem that way. In the same way "a swarm of insects at a distance seem to the eye like one body" or "as when the noise of many at a distance seems to the ear like a single voice." But in reality, to want riches, fame, or power is to want many things and those things change over time. (Yesterday's red-hot computer may be tomorrow's high-tech doorstop.)

In contrast, the pure of heart have only one goal: to see God. And Jesus promises them they will.

For us today

At first glance we might think this is the "sex" Beatitude—the equivalent of the commandment that says adultery is a sin.

It's easy for us to make that mistake because we tend to think of *pure* in the moral sense, as in no illicit hanky-panky. It does mean that, of course—fidelity in marriage and no sex outside marriage. But it isn't limited to that, anymore than a car is defined as only four wheels, an engine, or a transmission.

A car has all those things and more, bumper to bumper. To be morally pure includes our sexual conduct, certainly, but it has to do with our entire life style, from A to Z.

The broad meaning of the word *pure* comes out in some of the ways we use the term today. We want pure "chewing satisfaction" in our gum. We want pure milk chocolate in our candy bar. We want soap that, if not totally pure, is at least 99 and 44/100 percent that way.

Or at least advertisers tell us we do. And since their income depends on telling us things we like to hear—and they appear to be doing well financially—it would seem they are right.

We think pure is better than impure. Pure is better than tainted. Of course we do. And we don't necessarily trust our eyes or our noses or our taste buds when it comes to ensuring that we get the purity we demand. We buy filtering systems for our water taps to strain out any impurities that we might be drinking without even knowing it. We are concerned the consequences of those impurities will make themselves known in our health.

Are we fanatical? It might seem that way. We ask for a new fork at a restaurant if the one we're given isn't 100 percent clean. Why? Why not just scrape off that little bit of dried-on gunk and get on with the meal? After all, the rest of the fork, probably 95 percent or more, is fine. Why be so fussy?

Because we know that smidgen of crust could contain an untold number of germs. Because that fork has been in the mouth of a previous customer and we aren't about to put it in our own until it's been cleaned *completely*. Rinsed. Washed. Sanitized with extremely hot water and completely dried.

That's what this Beatitude is about. Jesus is saying we need to be just as fanatical, just as fussy, about how we live. We need hearts—beings, selves—that are clean. That are pure.

OK, but what's a pure lifestyle?

Well, how do we define it when we want something as simple as a drink of pure water? We want water that is clear and doesn't have any strange tints or opaqueness to it. We want water that is clean. No little chunks sinking to the bottom, no tiny flakes floating on the top. We want water that has no smell to it. We want water that tastes like, well, pure water.

But what does that taste like? If we've never had a glass of pure water how would we know it when we did come across one? The answer is the same—just as not-quite-satisfying and just as true—as the one we use in reply to "How do I know when I'm really in love?"

You'll know.

And once we taste that pure water (once we fall in true love), we discover there's nothing else like it. There is no substitute.

It can be the same with developing a pure heart, a clean heart. With water, once we begin to filter out the impurities, the chunks, the flakes, the smell, we begin to discover what it's *supposed* to taste like, and we fine-tune our senses so that we're more aware of the times it isn't like that. With our hearts, as we get rid of the chunks (our greed, for example), the flakes are more obvious (perhaps our anger).

The bad news, the hard news, is that this is a lifetime project. This is an ongoing challenge. That's because, to carry the analogy just one step further, our taps, our pipes, and our water system are corroded. We live in a sinful world. If we're not vigilant, if we don't purify what comes through that system, we're drinking water that isn't clean.

The good news, the encouraging news, is that the more we do this, the better we become at it. Our ability to do what is right grows stronger. And as it does, our ability to see God grows sharper.

So what?

Seeing God, that eternal beatific vision, is what we really want, even if we don't know it's what were missing. That's why, as Saint Augustine said, "Our hearts are restless until they rest in you."

But, as the first Beatitude told us, the kingdom of heaven isn't just something that will be, something into which we will be admitted later. It is now. It is here.

So where's God? If heaven is seeing God forever and we can participate in heaven now—even as we anticipate entering it later—where's God?

The temptation is to believe seeing God, finding God, is like the children's puzzle book "Where's Waldo?" Here is an intricate, complicated drawing, with dozens and dozens of people. Here is what Waldo looks like. Find him.

But it isn't like that. We live intricate, complicated lives on a planet with *billions* of people. Where's God? Find him.

What step did we just leave out? "Here is what God looks like." And what do we begin to understand as we strive to live a life of purity? That God looks like *us?* More. God is so much a part of our fellow humans, whatever we do for them, we do for him. Whatever we don't do for them, we're not doing for him.

The sixth Beatitude tells us that as our hearts become more pure, our vision clears and we can better see Jesus as he describes himself in the parable of the Last Judgment, as the one who is homeless, sick, in prison, and so on.

But *how* do we make our hearts more pure? The same way the apostles did. The same way the Fathers of the Church recommended. The same way the saints demonstrated in their own lives.

We do it by becoming better at prayer, a challenge which—not surprisingly—depends on our overcoming, pushing aside, avoiding, and running like crazy from sin—especially our old favorites, and we all have them. We all turn to them, falsely believing they will bring us comfort.

We do it by admitting that to see Jesus here on earth is to see Jesus suffering. And acknowledging that admission demands our action.

We do it by asking the help of the human most noted for her purity, for her faith, for her conforming her will to the will of God. By turning to Mary, the Mother of God.

And we do it by realizing and rejoicing in the fact that just as Jesus could touch a leper and make him clean, he can touch our hearts and do the same. By realizing he wants to do this. By realizing he is waiting for us to ask.

To read more about it

"Conference of Abba Isaac" by John Cassian in *The Catholic Tradition: Spirituality*, edited by the Rev. Charles Dollen, et al. (Wilmington, N.C.: McGrath Publishing, 1979)

Healing the Heart: The Transformational Power of Biblical Heart Imagery by Joseph A. Grassi. (New York: Paulist Press, 1987)

The Sanctifier by Luis M. Martinez, translated by Sister M. Aquinas, O.S.U. (Boston: St. Paul Editions, 1982)

Blessed are the peacemakers, for they will be called children of God

In Scripture

By the time Jesus came to his seventh Beatitude it must have been obvious to the crowd he was talking about big ideas. He was speaking of themes that were central to the history of the Hebrew people *and* to those right there, right then, listening to him talk.

Even some two thousand years later, the Jewish concept of peace is familiar to many Christians. The Hebrew word for peace, *shalom,* is one many Christians recognize.

A Bible concordance shows the word *peace* is used almost four hundred times throughout the Old and New Testament. In the New, the Greek word for *shalom, eirene,* is in every book. It's repeated eighty-eight times.

As with the fifth Beatitude's use of *mercy,* the English word *peace* doesn't do complete justice to the Hebrew or the Greek.

Shalom was much more than an absence of war. It also meant something was completed or finished, such as a debt. So it had to do with the lack of nothing, with perfection. It was also an everyday greeting, a way of saying hello.

Shalom was considered a gift from the Lord, and so there came to be a theological twist to the idea. But, even more than that, there was the concept "Yahweh is peace." When one was at peace, in a perfect state of well-being with others and himself or herself, then that person was in perfect sync with God.

And the peace the Lord bought could show itself in many ways. Rain in due season, great harvests, no enemies launching raids, and no wild animals attacking. To be at peace with

God was to be in a covenant with him and have him dwell among the people. Peace wasn't simply a group of folks who were fat and happy, it was a people living in righteousness, and in all that righteousness entails.

The opposite of peace was a bloody vengeance and with that came a curse (1 Kings 2:33).

The Chosen People longed for that perfect peace. They looked for their Messiah—their "Prince of Peace" (Isaiah 9:6).

In Christ's time, peace continued to be the common greeting. Today the celebrant welcomes the people at Mass with a greeting of peace. And again as is *mercy, peace* is a word that's sprinkled throughout Christian liturgical prayers. Perhaps it's so common, we sometimes fail to even notice it being said or even our saying it.

Jesus, the New Testament writers stressed, was the key to peace. "Peace I leave with you; my peace I give to you," he told his followers (John 14:27). "I do not give it to you as the world gives." God's peace cannot be matched by what the world offers. In fact, "the peace of God, which surpasses all understanding, will guard your hearts and minds in Christ Jesus," Saint Paul reminded the community at Philippi (Philippians 4:7).

But what about when Jesus told his apostles, "Do not think that I have come to bring peace to the earth; I have not come to bring peace but a sword" (Matthew 10:34). How does that square with the Prince of Peace and the gift he would be leaving them?

In this verse Scripture scholars tell us, the Greek *eirene* doesn't mean the same thing as the Hebrew *shalom*. Rather, here, *eirene* is used in the classical Greek sense. Jesus wasn't promising the absence of friction between his followers and all other people, not even within a family—"I have come to set a man against his father" (Matthew 10:35). The peace Jesus was bringing didn't mean freedom from persecution (which he went on to specifically mention in the next Beatitude). In fact, those who would try to accept and live Christ's peace would soon find themselves facing brutal opposition. There would be no relief until some three hundred years later (when the Roman Emperor Constantine saw to it Christianity was no longer outlawed).

This was his warning to his twelve apostles. It was at that same time he instructed them—before sending them out on what might be called their apostolic internship—to offer a greeting of peace, *shalom,* when they entered a house where they were going to stay. "If the house is worthy, let your peace come upon it," he said, "but if it is not worthy, let your peace return to you. If anyone will not welcome you or listen to your words, shake off the dust from your feet as you leave that house" (Matthew 10:13).

So more than simply a hello, they offered what Christ came to bring. They were giving an apostolic blessing, not unlike Yahweh's own— "So shall my word be that goes out from my mouth; it shall not return to me empty, but it shall accomplish that which I purpose, and succeed in the thing for which I sent it" (Isaiah 55:11). If the people in that house didn't accept an apostle's *shalom* (proving they weren't worthy of it), he was to take back that gift and move on. (Shaking the dust from one's feet was a Jewish gesture practiced in the Holy Land after taking a journey into "impure" pagan territory.)

So in this Beatitude is Jesus promising peace? No. He's talking about those who *make* peace. This isn't about someone simply being a recipient. It's about a person bringing about change. Accepting that blessing from Christ or one of his apostles and letting it act—come alive, grow, bear fruit—within him or her. It's about letting that blessing influence, motivate, and propel him or her into becoming someone who furthers the Kingdom of God on earth.

Jesus does not say "blessed are people who are peaceful" or "who are at peace." But "blessed are the ones who create peace." They are not passive but rather their activity, their lives bring God's *shalom.*

What's in store for them? They're going to be "called children of God."

To be called, meaning to become, a "son of God" (and in our own time, we would add "daughter of God") can be compared to being a "son of peace." A son of peace was peaceful. A son of justice was just. A son of God—or child of God—was to be like God, to be a person who was doing the work of God.

"Children of God" doesn't appear in the Old Testament but it's found fourteen times in the New. John begins his Gospel by explaining "to all who received him [Jesus], who believed in his name, he gave power to become children of God" (John 1:12).

Saint Paul, in his letter to the Romans, told Christ's followers "all who are led by the Spirit of God are children of God." "For you did not receive a spirit of slavery to fall back into fear," he continued, "but you have received a spirit of adoption. When we cry 'Abba! Father!' it is that very Spirit bearing witness with our spirit that we are children of God, and if children, then heirs, heirs of God and joint heirs with Christ— if, in fact, we suffer with him so that we may also be glorified with him" (Romans 8:14–17).

It is a title, a badge of honor and a reminder, Saint Paul uses elsewhere, too. "In Christ you are all the children of God through faith" (Galatians 3:26). And "Do all things without murmuring and arguing, so that you may be blameless and innocent, children of God without blemish in the midst of a crooked and perverse generation, in which you shine like stars in the world" (Philippians 2:14–15).

The promise was already being fulfilled. Those who made peace, who worked to live a life centered on God's peace, were his sons and daughters, heirs to an inheritance that included glory *through* suffering. They were stars shining in a crooked and perverse world.

Down through the ages

When the fifth century's Pope Saint Leo the Great (d. 461) was commenting on this Beatitude, he noted, "This blessedness, Dearly Beloved, is not promised to every kind of agreement, not to every sort of concord but to that of which the Apostle says: Let us have peace with God (Romans 5:1; Corinthians 8:11); and that of which the Prophet David says: Much peace have they that love the law; and to them there is no stumbling block (Psalm 119:165)."

This means, the pontiff taught, "the closest bond of friendship, the closest affinity of mind and heart, cannot truly claim this peace if these ties are not in conformity with the will of God."

How could a friendship *not* be in conformity with God's will?

"Excluded from the dignity of this peace," Saint Leo continued, "are they who are linked one with another by shameless desires, those joined together for the ends of crime and evil doing."

This is so because "there is no accord between the love of this world and the love of God" and "he shall not belong to the children of God who will not separate himself from the children of the world."

The peacemakers are the ones "who at all times have God in mind (Tobit 4:6), careful to keep the unity of the spirit in the bond of peace (Ephesians 4:3)." They "are never in conflict with the eternal law, saying in the prayer of faith: Thy will be done on earth as it is in heaven."

"These are the peacemakers," Saint Leo said. "These indeed are of one heart and mind, and dwell in holy harmony, and shall be called by the eternal name of sons of God, and joint heirs with Christ (Romans 8:17)."

And their final reward for loving God and neighbor will be to "suffer no more adversity, and go no more in fear of scandals, but with all the struggle of temptation at an end . . . rest in the most serene peace of God, through Jesus Christ our Lord, who with the Father and the Holy Spirit lives and reigns forever and ever. Amen."

Sixteenth-century Spanish Dominican
Bartolomé de Las Casas wrote about peace at
a time and place when war and conquest were
central. His father had accompanied Columbus
on his second voyage and Las Casas came to
the New World in 1502. From 1515 to 1522 he
fought the abuses of the colonial system and
promoted the peaceful colonization and evan-
gelization of the native people but had little
effect. A year later he entered the Dominicans
and went on with his work. In 1544 he was
named bishop of Chiapas (in what's now part
of Mexico).

"Violence cannot coerce the human will
into doing good," Las Casas wrote. "Nothing
contradicts consent more than force or fear —
and consent is the basis for judgment in good
faith. Approval of force or fear is immoral. And
there are certain transactions that require
express consent. Faith is one, and marriage,
baptism, voting, jurisdiction, etc."

Jesus, the bishop said, set the example of
attracting and converting people without the
use of force or fear. "The way was respectful,
attractive, altruistic, germane to humankind,"
he said. "He ordered that this be the way people should come under His gentle law, the way
the rest of the sinful world should be invited to
live under it also, very gently, very openly."

People need "peace, peace and quiet" to worship God, Las Casas said. "The souls of people cannot pay any attention to worshiping God in the conditions of panic, anxiety, unrest, and alarm—conditions that go with war."

Those circumstances fill a soul with "with terror, with pain and sorrow," with "things of that kind and many another which drives the soul to distraction" and makes it "incapable of doctrine and worship which demand peace."

That was why the "King of Peace . . . with pure compassion . . . ordered his followers to be peaceful, to be modest and kind."

The Holy Spirit "taught the prophet [Isaiah], the manner and means of forming the Kingdom of Christ," the Dominican wrote, and "the Christian people" the way to spread and preserve it. "Not by war. Not by force of arms. By the taste of peace. By an atmosphere of charity, by the works of kindness, of mercy, of modesty."

This has to be the way of "calling and convincing people to believe in Christ," he said. This means "clearly, it [is] ill-suited to the generosity, the kindness of Christ to subjugate to Himself, by war and its weaponry, any people, any kingdom."

That isn't how Christ drew people to himself; it isn't how the apostles furthered the Church. "There is a superb reason for this," Las

Casas said. "The weapons of war are physical things. Their nature is not to conquer souls but bodies, booty, buildings, material things they can reach. But it is through spiritual weapons that the Christian people are to be formed, gathered, settled, preserved—the way Christ wanted and still wants to gather, settle, expand, preserve those over whom He wanted a spiritual rule, so they might become His by faith, hope, charity, virtues of the free soul only."

In contrast, he said, the "spiritual arms" would include "a gospel message full of light, of gentleness, of kindness"; the sacraments; and "the grace of the Holy Spirit."

"These are the mighty weapons of Christ's army," the bishop wrote, "powerful enough to reach God, to reach the soul."

"Jesus forced no one," Las Casas stressed. "He took no one's property, or rights, or freedom. He deprived no one of wealth or rank by His primacy. He caused no one injury or trouble. He drew to Himself no one who was unwilling. He forced no one to submit to him after first striking terror into him with a weapon. People submitted to Christ the King avidly, viscerally, once they heard His words of eternal life, once they saw his miraculous deeds."

This was "how the Redeemer Himself began to form the Christian kingdom," the bishop said. "He laid the basis for its spread and its unity, gently, invitingly, appealing to free will. He left to each one the choice to kill the kingdom or to keep it. No force, no threat, no coercion on His part, no menace of war, so justice stayed intact."

In the twentieth century the founder of an ecumenical community has noted violence *must be* a facet of our peacemaking. "Every one of us, Christian or not, has violence in his make-up," wrote Brother Roger Schutz, who began the Taize community in France. "The only difference is the way we use it."

Some repress their feelings, he said, and "the result is pietistic passivity, a lack of any involvement on behalf of the victims of injustice." For them, "prayer is enough. Anything else might mean dirty hands."

At the other extreme, Brother Roger said, are the Christians who "want destructive violence or even, if it is effective, armed force."

"Could there be a third way, between passivity and destructive violence?" he asked. It's one we each have to discover for ourselves, he answered.

"Doing the will of God does not consist simply in saying 'Lord, Lord,'" Brother Roger wrote, "but in making a courageous contribution to the common good."

Neither, he continued, is peacemaking simply a matter of writing and signing petitions. "I know that some manifestos have at times had shock value," he said, "and have committed those who compromised themselves by signing them. But the very least we can say is that nowadays there are more than enough of them. So many people are canvassed to sign documents, to take sides for or against . . .

"Working out praiseworthy resolutions at the close of a meeting can lead to hypocrisy. We affirm in writing, we condemn, we appeal, and it all changes our lives not one bit. This procedure is rapidly becoming one of the diseases of the century."

Much better is the "violence of peacemakers."

"Violence of peacemakers!" Brother Roger exclaimed. "Could the whole spirit of the Gospel, capable of bringing revolution on this earth, be condensed in this apparent contradiction?

"It is not a question of just any kind of violence. The kind that takes hold of the Kingdom is creative. It does not bear the stamp of the need for power. . . . The violence of peacemakers!" he repeated. "It is a creative violence, revolutionizing people, and, by the challenge it presents, obliging them to take a stand."

This type of violence speaks to others, Brother Roger explained, and "can be recognized by certain signs." First, it is "like a living protest in the face of hardened Christian consciences, which accommodate themselves to hatred or to injustice." (It can be seen in those who oppose evil.)

Second, it is "a blaze of love," a "violence inhabited by a Presence." (The presence of God can be seen in it.)

Third, when a person's life is "ablaze in this way," he said, "he kindles a fire on the earth." (That love of God ignites the consciences of others.)

And fourth, he concluded, "it is a lifelong perseverance in intimacy with another life, the life of the Risen Christ." (It is a love of Jesus that endures despite hardships.)

If Christ "finds us faithful until death," he said, "he rewards our perseverance with an intimacy which fills our being and transmits life.

"Then we are granted the ability to discern beyond the world of things and events, beyond our transitory hopes, something much more intimate and much more profound. It is there that he awaits us."

For us today

The problem with saying "I am a Christian" is that it gives the impression that following Christ is a state of being. With this Beatitude, Jesus is saying it's an action.

"I am a Catholic" isn't supposed to be the same as "I am hungry" or "I am young" or "I am happy."

That's why this Beatitude isn't about "being at peace." It's about making peace happen. And peace—the peace of the kingdom—isn't furthered simply by our being, but by our doing.

Making this even more complex is the fact there can be a false peace and a true peace. Evil can make an agreement with evil to cooperate or to call a truce for a time but that isn't God's peace. For example, the classic "honor among thieves" (assuming there really is such a thing) is a peace based on expediency and fear. On the other hand, true peace is built on the integrity of our relationship with God.

That's why we can't really be making peace if we simply go along with the crowd when the crowd is going in the wrong direction. It's why making peace can mean standing firm in our beliefs despite adversities.

At times that involves being the "star" Saint Paul wrote about—the one shining in a "crooked and perverse" world. Light is an image that has been used countless times to describe the good person and the things he or she does, from Jesus' "you are the light of the world" (Matthew 5:14) to a recent president's "thousand points of light" recognition program. Even in the secular world, a person known and acknowledged by many others as talented is a "star."

Realizing it is "better to light one candle than curse the darkness"—to use the quotation made famous by The Christophers, a group that promotes Christian ideals—we need to come to understand that Jesus is calling us to *become* that candle, that light. We are called, with the grace of the Holy Spirit, to begin to transform ourselves into that "star."

And knowing now, scientifically, what Saint Paul had no way of knowing, we can see that other characteristics of a star, a heavenly body, also apply to the person who makes peace. A star can be defined as concentrated energy. It doesn't simply twinkle in the sky, it burns with an incredible intensity. Even after it has expired, after all that matter has been burned away, the light it produced continues on through the darkness of the cosmos. The light we see as we look into the night sky from our planet was made a long, long time ago.

In the same way, the good we do, the peace we make, can travel distances we can't even imagine. It can attract, intrigue, and inspire others to look for and find the Prince of Peace. It can change the lives—the hearts, the souls—of people we will never meet and never know about, until the day of Last Judgment when we learn how our actions have helped or hindered so many others.

And even after we are dead, after our "energy" is gone, the example we set, the life we lived, can be like the light from a star that no longer exists. The peace we made, having found a home in others, has become a part of their foundation in Christ, has become central to their own making of Christ's peace, has helped them become stars who are attracting, intriguing, and inspiring those among them still stumbling blindly in a crooked and perverse world.

We can do all that? Yes. We have the ability to make peace—to play a role in bringing that *shalom* to those "strangers," and, of course, to the people who live and work and play and pray around us.

In this Beatitude we are not called upon to placate everyone in our lives nor to avoid making waves at all costs, but to say and do what, as Christ's followers, we need to say and do.

Even in the secular sphere we're told this is the better way to live, not only for ourselves but for others. Not that we should be rude or brusque or hurtful, but we should be unflinchingly honest even when it initially hurts others (and, in a way, ourselves) to calmly and firmly state the truth. This is the key to the brutal but loving confrontation or intervention family and friends use to help someone who has a drinking or drug problem.

This is the key, we are told, to avoiding (or reversing) the role of "enabler"—the habitual lying about and accepting lies from an abuser, the continual avoiding, ignoring, and denying reality.

True peace within a family or friendship, within an individual who has a problem, will never come about without that honesty.

And doing that can be so hard! Few things in life are as difficult as no longer putting up with something that is wrong and destructive, something that is truly evil, and, instead, standing up to it. We must also recognize it is the sin—the continued alcohol abuse, for example—that is hated, not the sinner.

When we begin to make peace that way, begin to bring about true peace, we are called—we are becoming—"children of God."

And, it shouldn't surprise us that deep inside we feel very, very good the more we become God's children. Why is that so? Because the One who created us *made us in his image.* By our very nature—spiritual and temporal—we are designed to be like him.

To look like God. To think like God. To act like God. To love like God.

When we don't, we become the square peg trying to fit into the round hole. It simply doesn't work. It hurts, and the world offers a variety of excuses and remedies for that pain—for that emptiness and confusion—but, of course, none of them can satisfy and relieve us the way becoming that round peg can. Becoming that child of God.

And, again, our God loves us so much—has so much respect for us, has so much confidence in us—he *never* "shaves our corners" to make us fit. We always have free will. As Bartolomé de Las Casas stressed, God—and his Son Jesus— don't use force, except the force of invitation. The force of gentleness. The force of love.

We have the ability to become that round peg by choosing to become more like the One who is our creator. We can use our free will to choose to shave—to chisel off, to grind away, to sand down—those corners. And one of the ways we can do that is by becoming a person who makes peace.

But how do we make peace? We know the answers. The hard part is accepting them, believing them, putting them into practice in our daily lives.

To be a person of free will means that throughout our day, throughout our week, throughout our lives, we make choices that bring about peace or cause further division. It isn't simply that by the good things we do we become "more round." It's by the selfish things we do we become "more square."

To read more about it

Blessed Are the Peacemakers: Biblical Perspectives on Peace and Its Social Foundations edited by Anthony J. Tambasco (New York: Paulist Press, 1989)

New Testament Basis of Peacemaking by Richard T. McSorley (Scottsdale, Pa.: Herald Press, 1985)

The Only Way by Bartolomé de Las Casas, edited by Helen Rand Parish and translated by Francis Patrick Sullivan, S. J. (New York: Paulist Press, 1992)

Violent for Peace by Frère Roger of Taize (London: Mowbray, 1981)

Chapter 9

Blessed are those who are persecuted for righteousness sake, for theirs is the kingdom of heaven

In Scripture

J esus made no secret of the fact that his followers would be persecuted. "If they persecuted me, they will persecute you" (John 15:20). "They will arrest you and persecute you; they will hand you over to the synagogues and prisons" (Luke 21:12). "When they persecute you in one town, flee to the next" (Matthew 10:23).

The Jewish people were no strangers to persecution. They had known the oppression of slavery in Egypt and of exile and captivity in Babylon. Later, when Antiochus IV of Syria (ruled 175–164 B.C.) conquered Jerusalem, he tried to consolidate his power by forcing the Hebrews to worship Zeus. Those who refused were tortured and put to death. The story of those who resisted is told in the two Books of the Maccabees. An especially graphic and poignant description is given of the courage of one mother and her seven sons who were all tortured and killed on the same day (2 Maccabees 7:1–42).

Often enough in the Old Testament, persecution was the fate of those who witnessed to the word of God. In the case of the prophets, it was not an external power but their own government—their own people—who persecuted them when the people did not want to hear the prophets' words.

Elijah was forced to flee the country (1 Kings 17:9). At one point he lamented that he was the only prophet left: "I have been very zealous for the Lord, the God of hosts; for the Israelites have forsaken your covenant, thrown down your altars, and killed your prophets with the sword. I alone am left, and they are seeking my life, to take it away" (1 Kings 19:10).

When the princes of Judah were displeased with the prophetic words of Jeremiah, they had him thrown into a cistern (Jeremiah 38:6), and when King Jehoiakim disliked the words of the prophet Uriah, he "struck him down with the sword and threw his dead body into the burial place of the common people" (Jeremiah 26:23).

Zechariah spoke against the people for breaking the commandments, so "they conspired against him, and by command of the king they stoned him to death in the court of the house of the Lord" (2 Chronicles 24:20–21).

Not all the prophets were persecuted, but the New Testament certainly presents it as a fairly common occurrence. Stephen, the first martyr, asks those who were about to kill him, "Which of the prophets did your ancestors not persecute?" (Acts 7:51).

If the pattern had been to persecute and kill the prophets who spoke in the name of God, it continued in the case of Jesus, the greatest of prophets. Jesus seemed to realize this when he remarked "Yet today, tomorrow, and the next day, I must be on my way, because it is impossible for a prophet to be killed outside of Jerusalem. Jerusalem, Jerusalem, the city that kills the prophets and stones those who are sent to it! How often have I desired to gather your children together as a hen gathers her brood under her wings, and you were not willing" (Luke 13:33–34).

And that pattern of Jesus' life, foreshadowed in the prophets, would be true also of those who followed him and continued to speak the word of God.

The Acts of the Apostles tells the story of the persecution of the early Church. The apostles were flogged (Acts 5:40); the deacon Stephen was stoned to death (Acts 7:58); Christians were thrown into prison (Acts 8:3); and James was killed and Peter arrested (Acts 12:2–3).

Paul, who had once persecuted the Church, also spoke of his own sufferings: "Are they ministers of Christ? . . . I am a better one: with countless floggings, and often near death. Five times I have received from the Jews the forty lashes minus one. Three times I was beaten with rods. Once I received a stoning" (2 Corinthians 11:23–25).

The persecution of the prophets, those who spoke the word of God and who witnessed to Christ, continues throughout the New Testament.

The good news is that those who are persecuted for righteousness sake are blessed: "Blessed are you when people revile you and persecute you and utter all kinds of evil against you falsely on my account. Rejoice and be glad, for your reward is great in heaven, for in the same way they persecuted the prophets who were before you" (Matthew 5:11–12).

The good news is that Jesus is with those who are persecuted — so much so that he does not refer to the persecuted as "them," or "those folks over there," but as "me." "Saul, Saul, why do you persecute me?" (Acts 9:4).

The good news is that those who are persecuted for righteousness sake possess the kingdom of heaven. In this last beatitude, we are back to the theme of the kingdom, and we are back to the present tense. It is no longer that "*they will* be comforted," "they *will* inherit," "they *will* receive mercy." But "theirs *is* the kingdom of heaven."

What is the kingdom of heaven that the persecuted possess here and now? It is the very presence of Christ—the reality of Jesus in our midst, in our hearts. It both *is* and *is yet to come.* We know and love the Lord here and now, but our knowledge and love are not yet perfect. We are in the kingdom, we are in Christ, but we are still on the way—still growing in our love. "Now I know only in part; then I will know fully, even as I have been fully known" (1 Corinthians 13:12). "Beloved, we are God's children now; what we will be has not yet been revealed. What we do know is this: when he is revealed, we will be like him, for we will see him as he is" (1 John 3:2).

Aware of Christ's presence, aware of the kingdom, Jesus' followers found consolation even in the midst of persecution: "We are afflicted in every way, but not crushed; perplexed, but not driven to despair; persecuted, but not forsaken; struck down, but not destroyed" (2 Corinthians 4:8–9).

And they found the courage to continue to act as followers of Christ, as witnesses of his love: "When reviled, we bless; when persecuted, we endure; when slandered, we speak kindly" (1 Corinthians 4:12–13).

"All of you," Peter taught them, urged them, "have unity of spirit, sympathy, love for one another, a tender heart, and a humble mind. Do not repay evil for evil or abuse for abuse; but, on the contrary, repay with a blessing. It is for this that were you were called—that you might inherit a blessing" (1 Peter 3:8–9).

Down through the ages

Saint Cyprian understood the power of words, logic, and argument.

Born probably in Carthage, Africa, around 200, he had been a brilliant pagan rhetorician, lawyer, and teacher before being baptized in 246. Then, filled with a convert's zeal, he focused his talents on learning about and defending the Church. (Later he was ordained a priest, then made a bishop before being martyred in 258.)

Saint Cyprian had a bone to pick with those who were persecuting Christians. He claimed their actions made no sense.

"What is this insatiable madness for blood-shedding, what [is] this interminable lust of cruelty?" he demanded of them.

"Rather," he argued, "make your election of one of two alternatives. To be a Christian is either a crime, or it is not. If it is a crime, why do you not put the man that confesses it to death? If it be not a crime, why do you persecute an innocent man?"

Why, he wanted to know, if a Christian doesn't try to hide the fact he is a Christian, do the authorities torture him like someone who is accused of a crime but refuses to admit his guilt until the pain forces him to confess?

Christians, he emphasized, freely and openly admit they are "guilty" of believing in Jesus.

And, he pointed out, "none of us, when he is apprehended, makes resistance, nor avenges himself against your unrighteous violence, although our people are numerous and plentiful."

There had not been, and would not be, any Christian "uprising," he said. Rather, the followers of Jesus believed God would deal with and avenge those who persecuted them.

Christians "are never prostrated by adversity," Saint Cyprian told his pagan audience, "nor are we broken down, nor do we grieve or murmur in any external misfortune or weakness of body: living by the Spirit rather than by the flesh, we overcome bodily weakness by mental strength. By those very things which torment and weary us, we know and trust that we are proved and strengthened."

For the present, he said, "good and evil" people are "contained in the same household"; they live in the same world, but that doesn't mean they "suffer adversity" in the same way. "Among you there is always a clamorous and complaining impatience," he said. "With us there is a strong and religious patience, always quiet and always grateful to God. . . . There flourishes with us the strength of hope and the firmness of faith."

Even during times of persecution, he noted, "among these very ruins of a decaying world, our soul is lifted up, and our courage unshaken. . . . [Christians] always exult in the Lord, and rejoice and are glad in their God; and the evils and adversities of the world they bravely suffer, because they are looking forward to gifts and prosperities to come."

At the same time, that's not to say Christians *want* to suffer. In prayer, "we always ask for the repulse of enemies," Cyprian said, "and either for the removal or the moderating of adversity."

But that wasn't all they prayed for. Saint Cyprian said the Christian community was praying for those who were torturing and killing them. "We pour forth our prayers, and, propitiating and appeasing God, we entreat constantly and urgently, day and night, for your peace and salvation."

He offered his adversaries "the wholesome help of our mind and advice." "Because we may not hate," he wrote, "and we please God more rendering no return for wrong, we exhort you while you have the power, while there remains to you something of life, to make satisfaction to God, and to emerge from the abyss of darkling superstition into the bright light of true religion."

In other words, please join us while you still can.

"We do not envy your comforts," Saint Cyprian told them, "nor do we conceal divine benefits. We repay kindness for your hatred; and for the torments and penalties which are inflicted on us, we point out to you the ways of salvation."

The sixteenth-century French theologian and church reformer John Calvin wanted it made clear Christians don't *enjoy* suffering, nor are they indifferent to it.

"Patiently to bear the cross is not to be utterly stupefied and to be deprived of all feeling of pain," Calvin wrote. Christians are not "Stoics of old."

"We have nothing to do with this iron philosophy," he taught, "which our Lord and Master has condemned not only by his word, but also by his example. For he groaned and wept both over his own and others' misfortune. And he taught his disciples in the same way: 'The world,' he says, 'will rejoice: but you will be sorrowful and weep' (John 16:20)."

And, Calvin said, Jesus also was afraid, just as the early martyrs were.

Christians "willingly and cheerfully" undergo persecution, the theologian said, but that doesn't mean this Christian cheerfulness takes away pain's sting.

"Otherwise," he pointed out, "in the cross there would be no forbearance of the saints unless they were tormented by pain and anguished by trouble."

If they liked being persecuted where was the sacrifice?

"If there were no harshness in poverty," he continued, "no torment in disease, no sting in disgrace, no dread in death—what fortitude or moderation would there be in bearing them with indifference? But since each of these, with an inborn bitterness, by its very nature bites the hearts of us all, the fortitude of the believing man is brought to light if—tried by the feelings of such bitterness—however grievously he is troubled with it, yet valiantly resisting, he surmounts it. . . . If wounded by sorrow and grief, he rests in the spiritual consolation of God."

In our own time, Salvadoran Archbishop Oscar Romero is an example of someone who brought persecution on himself by becoming an advocate for those who were being persecuted.

Although "frequently . . . threatened with death," he continued to promote peace and human rights in El Salvador.

But, Romero noted, "as a Christian, I do not believe in death but in resurrection." And, "as a pastor," he was "bound by a divine command to give my life for those whom I love." That, he added, "includes all Salvadorans, even those who are going to kill me."

To be martyred "is a grace from God that I do not believe I have earned," Romero said. "But if God accepts the sacrifice of my life, then may my blood be the seed of liberty, and a sign of the hope that will soon become a reality."

"You can tell them," he said, "if they succeed in killing me, that I pardon them, and I bless those who may carry out the killing."

And then he added, "But I wish that they would realize that they are wasting their time. A bishop will die, but the church of God—the people—will never die."

On March 24, 1980, Romero was shot and killed while celebrating Mass.

Prior to his death, the archbishop taught "the Church has never incited to hatred or revenge, not even at those saddest of moments when priests have been murdered and faithful Christians have been killed or have disappeared [been kidnapped and never seen again]."

In spite of this, he wrote, the Church "has continued to preach Jesus' command 'love one another' (John 15:12)."

It must. The Church can't renounce that command, he said, and it hasn't. "On the contrary, it has recalled that other command, 'pray for those who persecute you' (Matthew 5:44)."

For us today

The persecution of Christians can seem remote—a different place, if not a different era.

Yes, persecutions happened in the first centuries after Christ. Yes, they are happening today in countries under totalitarian regimes.

But for us here and now? No. They were back then. They are over there.

It's easy to fail to see how we are connected to those people. How we are indebted to them.

Catholics today are reaping a harvest planted centuries ago by the men, women, and even children who had the courage and the faith to die rather than denounce their belief in Jesus. They had the courage to be tortured—sometimes as a lesson to other citizens, sometimes simply for sport—rather than consent to say a prayer to a pagan god or offer a few grains of incense in its honor.

It was Tertullian (c. 160–c. 225) who said "The blood of the martyrs is the seed of the Church." Those seeds, their blood, over time have become our roots.

And the seeds continue to be planted. Those today—like Archbishop Romero, who are tortured and killed for righteousness, for justice, for the Gospel—continue to plant seeds of Christian faith, "the seed of liberty and a sign of hope."

Why do these Catholics continue to be persecuted? Because they continue to live the Gospel. They refuse to live a life that is not righteous, that does not seek justice for everyone, including the poorest, the weakest, the most ignored and forgotten.

They refuse to live a life that is not centered on Christ who continues to remind us "I was hungry; I was thirsty; I was in prison." They refuse to stop being a Christian, which means they refuse to stop acting as Christ, who reached out to the poor, the outcast, the lepers, the sinners.

Their lives and example are a challenge to us. If the prophets are always persecuted and we find that we are *not* persecuted what does this tell us about our own prophetic witness?

Are we aware enough of the situation of our own time to be witnesses for Christ? Do we know what's happening? Do we recognize and acknowledge the suffering around us? Or are we so caught up in our own concerns and so self-centered that we have eyes but don't see and ears but don't hear? Do we remain ignorant but not innocent because we skipped that newspaper article, we flipped the channel when that report began, we didn't bother to inform ourselves about the issues in that election?

If we are to be prophets, we need to know what's happening, to educate ourselves about how the political actions of our country—and our own buying habits—have an impact on the lives of citizens of other lands.

Only then can we support those leaders who champion the rights—including the religious rights—of others and oppose those who promote a domestic or foreign policy motivated by greed, prejudice, fear, bigotry, anger, racism, sin.

Are we aware and, if we are aware, are we willing to act and willing to speak? Say we're at a staff meeting and get an idea about the ethics of present company policy. Perhaps a suggestion that will identify us as a Christian, a suggestion that will let everyone know our values and what we stand for. Do we propose it? Do we take the risk? Face the possible hassle?

Or maybe we're on the sidelines watching our child play soccer and notice other parents avoiding one extremely unpopular dad who's obnoxious and abrasive. Will we talk with him or join the smug crowd who's decided to give him the cold shoulder? Will we risk alienating the parents we do like?

Or around the neighborhood, do we let people know what we believe or avoid mentioning it because we don't want to be known as a "religious" person? Why not? Perhaps because the entertainment industry continues to hammer home the message anyone who professes to believe in God is crazy or hypocritical. Do we speak when the opportunity is there or stay silent?

The price of our witness may be small in comparison to what others have suffered and are suffering for their faith. But are we willing to take even that risk and endure that inconvenience? Are we willing to endure the co-worker who might snicker, the friend who might be a bit miffed, the neighbor who might gossip and joke about us?

If we find that we face no persecution—that no one ever gets upset with us because of what we believe—then maybe it's because we never show, never say, what we believe. Not all are called to be martyrs and give their lives for their faith. But all are called to be witnesses, to be prophets. And the prophet is never popular with everyone.

Our faith grows from the seed of the martyrs. We are guided, built up, strengthened by the example of those who have gone before us in the Church and the example of those suffering now. Is anyone built up by our own example? By our own witness? By our own willingness to take risks for our faith?

"If they have persecuted me, they will persecute you." Since the time of Christ each of his followers has been asked to give witness, to take up his or her own cross and follow.

It's no different today.

To read more about it

Job and the Mystery of Suffering: Spiritual Reflections by Richard Rohr (New York: Crossroad, 1996)

On the Christian Meaning of Human Suffering (Salvifici Doloris) by Pope John Paul II (Washington, D.C.: United States Catholic Conference, 1984)

Suffering and Martyrdom in the New Testament by William Horbury and Brian McNeil (Cambridge: Cambridge University Press, 1981)

Living the Beatitudes today

With the "kingdom of heaven" in the eighth Beatitude, we come full circle. We began with a promise of the kingdom to the poor in spirit and end with that same promise, now to those who suffer persecution for righteousness sake.

The next two verses explain the last promise a bit more and make it more challenging and immediate as they switch from third to second person—from "they" to "you": "Blessed are you when people revile you and persecute you and utter all kinds of evil against you falsely on my account. Rejoice and be glad, for your reward is great in heaven, for in the same way they persecuted the prophets who were before you."

It's a handy literary device to end a discourse the same way it began. We still use it today in writing and speaking, and it's not uncommon in Scripture. (Another example is Matthew 6:6–11, which begins and ends with a warning to "beware of the yeast of the Pharisees and Sadducees.")

But perhaps this literary device can also tell us something about living the Beatitudes. Maybe by following the Beatitudes, we "come full circle" in more ways than one.

As the circle is one, though made of many points, so the Beatitudes are somehow one. They're interrelated, interconnected, overlapping. What Jesus was saying about being poor in spirit has to do with being a peacemaker. Being meek is connected to being merciful. Striving to lead a life that is righteous means being persecuted in some way, large or small, because of that.

Like facets of a single diamond, the Beatitudes are ways of living and reflecting a single love. In the Sermon on the Mount, Jesus holds up the gem for all to see and turns it in the sunlight so that each side sparkles. To live the Beatitudes is to let God's love be reflected in all the many facets of our lives.

When we trace a circle, we begin at a single point and eventually return there again. When we live the Beatitudes, we stretch the circle of our lives out into the world and back again to the place of our beginning. The Beatitudes draw us out and draw us back—out into the world and back into the presence of God within us.

To live the Beatitudes is to be active and aware in the world. Finding ways to be peacemakers, to bring reconciliation. Seeking out opportunities for mercy and compassion. Pursuing justice and righteousness as a hunger and a thirst.

We live the Beatitudes where we are right now. We live them one decision, one action at a time.

We live them realizing we are imperfect, we make mistakes, we need forgiveness.

We live them with confidence in Jesus' promise of a joy and peace that only God can give.

And in our attempt to live the Beatitudes, we become more aware of who we really are and where we should be going. That we are a people born of God's love, and we are on our way to the fullness of that love. That we are called to be (and should continue to become) the meek, the pure in heart, the poor in spirit, the *anawim*—the little ones of Yahweh.

As the Beatitudes end where they began—with the kingdom of God—they lead us back to our beginning. And they point us toward our final goal in that same kingdom, in the very heart of God.

Sources

Albert the Great, "Ennarrationes in Evangelium Matthaei," in Benedict Viviano, O.P., *The Kingdom of God in History* (Wilmington, Del.: M. Glazier, 1988).

Anthony of Padua, Seek First His Kingdom (Padua: Conventual Franciscan Friars, 1988).

Augustine, "Commentary on the Lord's Sermon on the Mount," and "Sermon 53: On the Beatitudes" in *The Fathers of the Church: A New Translation,* Denis J. Kavanagh, O.S.A., trans. (New York: Fathers of the Church, Inc., 1951).

Bartolomé de Las Casas, *The Only Way,* Helen Rand Parish, ed., Francis Patrick Sullivan, S.J., trans. (New York: Paulist Press, 1992).

Dietrich Bonhoeffer, *The Cost of Discipleship* (New York: Macmillan, 1968).

The Book of Catholic Quotations, John Chapin, ed. (New York: Farrar, Straus and Cudahy, 1956).

Caesarius of Arles, "Sermon 25" in *Corpus Christianorum* (Turnholti: Typographi Brepols, 1953).

Catechism of the Catholic Church (Liguori, Mo.: Liguori Publications, 1994).

John Calvin, *Institutes of the Christian Religion* (London: SCM Press, 1961).

Catherine of Siena, *The Dialog,* Susanne Noffke, O.P., trans. (New York: Paulist Press, 1980).

John Chrysostom, "Homilies on the Sermon on the Mount" in *The Preaching of Chrysostom,* J. Pelikan, ed., (Philadelphia: Fortress, 1967).

John Cassian, "Conferences of Abba Isaac" in *The Catholic Tradition: Spirituality,* Rev. Charles Dollen, et al. eds. (Wilmington, N.C.: McGrath Publishing Co., 1979).

Cyprian, "An Address to Demetrianus" in vol. 5 of *The Ante-Nicene Fathers,* A. Roberts and J. Donaldson, eds. (Grand Rapids, Mich.: Wm B. Eerdmans Publishing Co., 1981).

Cyril of Jerusalem, Catechetical Lectures quoted in Berard Marthaler, *The Creed* (Mystic, Conn.: Twenty-third Publications, 1993).

The Documents of Vatican II, William M. Abbot, S.J., ed. (New York: Guild Press, 1966).

Gregory of Nyssa, "On the Beatitudes, Sermon 3" in *From Glory to Glory: Texts from Gregory of Nyssa's Mystical Writings*, Herbert Musurillo, trans. and ed. (New York: Scribners, 1961).

Pope John Paul II, *On the Permanent Validity of the Church's Missionary Mandate* (Redemptoris missio) (Washington, D.C.: U.S. Catholic Conference, 1990).

Julian of Norwich, *Revelations of Divine Love* (New York: Penguin, 1966).

Søren Kierkegaard, "Purity of Heart: Edifying Discourses in Various Spirits," in *A Kierkegaard Anthology*, R. Bretall, ed. (New York: Modern Library, 1946).

Martin Luther King Jr., "Our God is Able" and "Pilgrimage to Nonviolence," in *Strength to Love* (New York: Harper & Row, 1963).

Leo the Great, Sermon XCV, "Homilia de gradibus ascensionis ad beatitudinem," in *Sunday Sermons of the Great Fathers*, M. F. Toal, trans. and ed. (Chicago: Henry Regnery, 1963).

Martin Luther, "Temporal Authority" in *Selected Political Writings: Luther*, J. M. Porter, ed. (Philadelphia: Fortress Press, 1974).

Jürgen Moltmann, *The Theology of Hope* (New York: Harper, 1967).

Origen, "Commentary on Matthew," quoted in "Royaume de Dieu" in *Dictionnaire de Spiritualité ascétique et mystique, doctrine et histoire* (Paris: Beauchesne, 1988).

Frère Roger of Taize, *Violent for Peace* (London: Mowbray, 1981).

Oscar Romero, "Second Pastoral Letter" in *Voice of the Voiceless* (Maryknoll, N.Y.: Orbis, 1990).

———. *La Voz De Los Sin Voz: La Palabra Viva De Monsenor Oscar Arnulfo Romero* (San Salvador: UCA, 1980).

Mother Teresa, *Mother Teresa: Contemplative in the Heart of the World* (Ann Arbor, Mich.: Servant Books, 1985).

Therese of Lisieux, *The Autobiography of St. Therese of Lisieux: The Story of A Soul* (Garden City, N.Y.: Image, 1957).

Thomas Aquinas, *Summa Theologica* (New York: Beniziger, 1946).

Vincent de Paul, *Correspondence, Entretiens, Documents* (Paris: Librairie Lecoffre, 1924).

John Wesley, "Upon Our Lord's Sermon on the Mount" in *The Works of John Wesley* (Grand Rapids, Mich.: Zondervan, 1958).

Index